Curriculum Reform in the European Schools

Sandra Leaton Gray • David Scott
Peeter Mehisto

Curriculum Reform in the European Schools

Towards a 21st Century Vision

Sandra Leaton Gray
UCL Institute of Education
London, UK

David Scott
UCL Institute of Education
London, UK

Peeter Mehisto
UCL Institute of Education
London, UK

ISBN 978-3-030-10062-9   ISBN 978-3-319-71464-6 (eBook)
https://doi.org/10.1007/978-3-319-71464-6

© The Editor(s) (if applicable) and The Author(s) 2018 This book is an open access publication.
Softcover re-print of the Hardcover 1st edition 2018
Open Access This book is licensed under the terms of the Creative Commons Attribution 4.0 International License (http://creativecommons.org/licenses/by/4.0/), which permits use, sharing, adaptation, distribution and reproduction in any medium or format, as long as you give appropriate credit to the original author(s) and the source, provide a link to the Creative Commons license and indicate if changes were made.
The images or other third party material in this book are included in the book's Creative Commons license, unless indicated otherwise in a credit line to the material. If material is not included in the book's Creative Commons license and your intended use is not permitted by statutory regulation or exceeds the permitted use, you will need to obtain permission directly from the copyright holder.
The use of general descriptive names, registered names, trademarks, service marks, etc. in this publication does not imply, even in the absence of a specific statement, that such names are exempt from the relevant protective laws and regulations and therefore free for general use.
The publisher, the authors and the editors are safe to assume that the advice and information in this book are believed to be true and accurate at the date of publication. Neither the publisher nor the authors or the editors give a warranty, express or implied, with respect to the material contained herein or for any errors or omissions that may have been made. The publisher remains neutral with regard to jurisdictional claims in published maps and institutional affiliations.

Cover illustration: © Zoonar GmBH / Alamy

Printed on acid-free paper

This Palgrave Macmillan imprint is published by the registered company Springer International Publishing AG part of Springer Nature.
The registered company address is: Gewerbestrasse 11, 6330 Cham, Switzerland

Foreword

I once had the honour of sitting at a reception table next to Mr. Albert Van Houtte, one of the founding fathers of the European Schools. By this time he was already over ninety years old, but crystal clear in his thinking and somewhat straightforward in his mode of expression. He peered at me, slowly shaking his head, and commented: 'Listen, young man. I am really disappointed. We drafted the basis of the European school system in a hurry. It took us only a few weeks to sort it out. Now, fifty years later, you have not managed to change and develop it in any way whatsoever!'

He was right. The basic principles of the European School system had remained intact for sixty years. In the same time the world around the European schools had completely changed. The European Union itself had grown from 6 to 28 member states, the number of languages and language sections had quadrupled, and the organisation of the schools had become more and more complex, without even speaking about the ongoing pressure to reform the curriculum in order to meet the educational needs of the youngsters of the twenty-first century.

As Secretary-General of the European School system I made it a priority to launch a wholescale reform of the system. The Board of Governors of the European schools created a working group to discuss the matter. It was obvious that an external view was needed. That important task was given to the Institute of Education, University College London. The group of experts from the UCL Institute of Education came up with a rather impressive array of essential and well-justified remarks and recommendations, as you will see from the contents of this book.

Many of these recommendations are not only valid for the European school system but they have a greater, universal value. What should an ideal twenty-first century curriculum look like? What are the aims and objectives of a modern educational programme? How should we implement the eight EU key competences in the curriculum design? How should we create a coherent and effective educational setting? What kind of skills and competences will students need for successful entry to further and higher education? What is the role of the mother tongue in a multilingual and multicultural context? What would be the best way to promote language teaching? How should we develop assessment and evaluation standards? This is just a sample of the many questions that need to be raised.

After the presentation of the UCL Institute of Education report's concepts, ideas and recommendations, it became clear to us that it was necessary to launch a deep consultation and reflection debate within the schools and with the stakeholders in order to decide which reform path to follow. In the light of this, I addressed the following letter to the entire European school community:

> Dear All
>
> For over 60 years, the objective of the European Schools has been to provide a broad education of high quality, from nursery school to university entrance, offering our pupils an opportunity to be educated through their Mother Tongue, whilst being immersed in a multilingual and multicultural environment, in order to become open-minded European citizens. We are convinced that this objective is still valid today – but it might be worthwhile revising and updating our curriculum and some of our practices, taking into account the demands of the twenty first century that our students are facing.
>
> This autumn the *Reorganisation of Secondary Cycle Studies Working Group* will discuss the secondary school curriculum based on earlier discussions and proposals, but also taking into account the recommendations made by the external evaluator, the Institute of Education, University College London. According to the report of the team of evaluators, current practice,

as well as the new proposals, do not take sufficient account of, for example, the eight key competences.

One of the key messages of the final evaluation report of the Institute of Education, University College London is that we should 'clarify and extend the current outline curriculum, particularly in relation to the eight key competences'. Indeed, the European Schools should be at the forefront in translating these European key competences into learning and teaching practices.

According to the same report, the most important component of curriculum reform is improving teacher capacity. This can be achieved in two ways:

1. recruiting teachers who already have the requisite knowledge base, skills and dispositions, or/and
2. developing pre- and in-service training programmes to compensate for the lack of knowledge, skills and dispositions required to teach the new syllabuses.

During the summer I participated in a Curriculum Confrontation Event entitled *What's worth learning?* I learned from the various stakeholders, that:

- all the 28 European countries have revised/reformed their curricula during the last decade;
- the world in which our Schools operate has undergone major changes in the past twenty years: increasing globalisation and challenges for a sustainable future are only two examples;
- the set of competences a pupil should master has changed to include cross-curricular, ethical and sustainability elements.
- the concept of learning has evolved. It is important to strengthen the importance of learning to learn. That ability should be embedded in basic skills such as literacy, numeracy and ICT, which are necessary for continuous learning. An individual should therefore be able to acquire, access, profess and assimilate new knowledge and new skills. Students should also be able to learn autonomously, be self-disciplined, work collaboratively, share what they have learned, organise their own learning, evaluate their own work, seek advice, information and support when appropriate;

- the role of teachers and of teaching has also changed: we are moving towards a school as a learning community; and
- the content of syllabuses and pedagogical practices should take into consideration the cross-subject issues of our environment, so that students are able to deal with real problems and real-world phenomena.

We should also take time to reflect on how to make our schools a better learning environment and a more supportive and encouraging community, which enhances the meaningfulness of studying at school. The motivation and well-being of our staff members as well as the joy in learning of our students should be promoted. All these pedagogical issues will be discussed in various forums during this school year.

I invite the entire European School community to take part in the discussion.

Brussels, 9th September 2015

Kari Kivinen
Secretary-General of the European Schools

The reform process of the European school system is still ongoing. The UCL recommendations changed profoundly the scope of the reform and gave a broader vision and new direction to our school system development approach. The curriculum design ideas proposed by the UCL multi-disciplinary expert team were based on new developments in pedagogy and on the latest educational research findings. Their report linked educational research theory with the everyday practice of schooling in a holistic way.

School providers, school heads, teachers, parents and political policy-makers all over Europe are confronted with the same questions as we are in the European schools. How can we reform the school system to provide students with the right set of competences for the future? How can we bring new findings of the pedagogical research into practice? How can we build up a differentiated curriculum, which takes account of the different types of needs and abilities of children? How can we reform assessment systems to meet the new challenges of increased accountability?

This book is an intellectually stimulating overview of the latest curriculum design ideas of pedagogical research. It will be of interest to everybody who wants to grasp the essence of the ideal twenty-first century educational setting, according to the leading academics in the field.

Brussels, Belgium Kari Kivinen

Acknowledgements

A team of researchers from University College London, Institute of Education, carried out the research for this book during the academic year 2014–2015, as part of a European Commission funded evaluation project looking specifically at the upper secondary phase of education in the European Schools System (cf. Leaton Gray et al. 2015). The team comprised Sandra Leaton Gray, David Scott, Didac Gutierrez-Peris, Peeter Mehisto, Norbert Pachler and Michael Reiss.

Reference

Leaton Gray, S., Scott, D., Gutierrez-Peris, D., Mehisto, P., Pachler, N. and Reiss, M. (2015) *External Evaluation of a Proposal for the Reorganisation of Secondary Studies in the European School System*, London: UCL Institute of Education.

Contents

1 Becoming Europeans: A History of the European Schools   1

2 Acquainted with All that Is Great and Good:
   Designing a Twenty-First Century Curriculum   23

3 Educated Side by Side: The Role of Language
   in the European Schools   49

4 A United and Thriving Europe? A Sociology
   of the European Schools   75

5 Schooled and Ready: Assessment Reform   99

6 Consolidating the Work of Their Fathers: Moving
   on from European Schools to Higher Education   121

7 Belonging Together: A Model for Education
   in a New European Age   139

References   161

Author Index   175

Subject Index   179

List of Tables

Table 1.1	Category I European Schools	5
Table 1.2	Pupil population by nationality and by national populations	13
Table 1.3	Pupil population from 2013 to 2016	15
Table 2.1	An option-less curriculum	39
Table 2.2	An option within pathways curriculum	40
Table 2.3	Current arrangement of subjects S1–S5	42
Table 2.4	S6–S7 Current arrangement of studies (i.e. last two years of secondary education)	43
Table 6.1	University College London Undergraduate Degrees	133
Table 6.2	University of Luxembourg Undergraduate Degrees	134
Table 6.3	University of Barcelona Undergraduate Degrees	135

1

Becoming Europeans: A History of the European Schools

Educated side by side, untroubled from infancy by divisive prejudices, acquainted with all that is great and good in the different cultures, it will be borne in upon them as they mature that they belong together. Without ceasing to look to their own lands with love and pride, they will become in mind Europeans, schooled and ready to complete and consolidate the work of their fathers before them, to bring into being a united and thriving Europe. (Jean Monnet 1953)

The European Schools were founded nearly sixty years ago in the aftermath of World War Two, with the first being established in Luxembourg, which, together with Brussels and Strasbourg, is one of the three official capitals of the European Union and the seat of the European Court of Justice. There are now fourteen schools in seven countries serving over 25,000 students. Designed for the children of European Union employees, they have a special legal status within Europe and use a particular model of curriculum and assessment that in many ways represents a hybrid of the different European educational models in existence. In this book we examine the role, function and status of these European schools.

It is customary to speak of a group of schools as a *system* and indeed there is a great deal of sense in this for the reasons we explain below. However, describing education as a system risks ignoring the core of that activity, namely, that it is a series of profoundly personal acts of learning. Thus from the outset, any consideration of this education system also needs to take into account the tension between the instinctive drive to learn and the systematic attempt to organize and control it. The root of this tension lies in the difference between the basic demand for access to learning opportunities for the satisfaction of needs (emotional, spiritual, material and intellectual) and the selection and control processes that education systems undertake.

Education systems change over time and experience alterations to both their internal and external structures and relations. Whether change occurs or not depends on the capacity within the system as well as the condition of the change-catalyst or set of reforms. And these in turn are structured in particular ways, which determines their ability to act as change-agents. Certain types of catalyst are more likely to induce change in a system than others; for example, changes of personnel (caused naturally through retirements and deaths or by people in powerful positions within the system exercising their authority), new policies, events in nature, external interventions, new arrays of resources, new arrangements of roles and functions within a system, new financial settlements and so forth. In short, some of these change-catalysts are more powerful than others, or at least have the potential to be more powerful. Even here though, the capacity of the catalyst to effect change within a system cannot guarantee or determine whether change actually occurs. We can see this most clearly in some of the reform processes undertaken in the European School System, such as the 2009 reforms which focused on opening up the system and the European Baccalaureate to other students, governance issues in the system, and cost-sharing amongst the member states. Any reform or change process does not guarantee or determine the degree of change within the system, how long lasting the reform is and any unexpected consequences that occur. Furthermore, some types of change-catalyst are more likely to be successful in inducing change within the system than others. This is not only because some interventions in education systems are more powerful than others but also because their capacity to induce change fits better the change mechanism within the system being reformed.

For example, in a system that has a high level of command structure between the coordinating body and its constituent parts, a policy for change at the classroom level that is underpinned by a strong system of rewards and sanctions is likely to be successful in inducing change at this level. This is in contrast to systems which grant greater degrees of autonomy to their teachers, and consequently the same change mechanism may have less chance of succeeding. Extra-national change-agents work in the same way and the Organisation for Economic Cooperation and Development's system of international assessment (known as the Programme for International Student Assessment) is an example of this. What these globalizing bodies, such as the OECD, are attempting to do is establish a form of global panopticism where the activities of the various national and cross-national systems are made visible to a supra-national body, with the consequence that all parts of the system are visible from one single point. However, what this needs is a single surface of comparison or at least a comparative mechanism that can do this, so that enough people have confidence in it for it to be considered useful. This fundamentally applies to a particular education system, such as the European School System, which is the focus of this book.

What we have been doing here is categorizing the European School System as a set of institutions and relations between its parts, and even perhaps as a coordinating body for a number of sub-systems, which have a particular relation to the central authority and a particular position within it. However, this doesn't mean that relations between the central authority and the schools, and in addition, between the system and other bodies external to it, remain the same over time. These relations may change for a number of possible reasons, for example, the invention of new ideas, natural progression, contradictions as historically accumulating structural tensions between open activity systems (cf. Engeström 2001) and so forth.

It is fairly easy to understand an education system as a coordinating body that directs a number of sub-units, so that if the central authority demands action of a particular type, then these subsidiary bodies will implement its directives. The cohering element in the notion of a system being used here is that one body commands a series of other bodies, though all of them are considered to be elements of a system. However, it is rare for any actual system to function in this way. Within the system the extent and type of power that the coordinating body can exercise over the other elements may be exercised in different ways. Thus, a system's coordinating body may have less or more direct relations with different parts of the system. Indeed, it may be that some of these relations become so attenuated that it becomes harder to include them in the system.

Furthermore, systems have internal rules, that is, their elements are arranged in particular ways. Traditional systems have a high degree of specialization; a clearly defined division of labour; the distribution of official tasks within the organization; a hierarchical structure of authority with clearly defined areas of responsibility; formal rules which regulate the operation of the organization; a written administration; a clear separation between what is official and what is personal; and the recruitment of personnel on the basis of ability and technical knowledge. All of this is relevant to the European School System, so long as it is understood that this system was set up with a particular purpose in mind and a set of accountability relations to a central authority, the European Union Commission, which means that its bureaucratic structures are particular to that system.

However, regardless of how we understand the notion of a system, any change to it is always a transformation of the status quo, to a greater or lesser degree. Therefore, we need to understand how those systems and curricula are and have been structured. What this means is that the same programme of reform delivered in different systems of education is likely to have different effects on the different elements of the system and will have different histories within the system. In the first instance then we are concerned to plot the history of this almost unique education system.

A History of the European School System

The European School System was formed in October 1953 in Luxembourg, and was the initiative of members of the European Coal and Steel Community and the Luxembourg Government. The six different governments of the Community and their respective ministries of education worked together to forge a system that educated pupils with different mother tongue languages and different nationalities. In April 1957, the signing of the Protocol made the Luxembourg school the first official European school. The first European Baccalaureate was awarded in July 1959 and the qualification was recognised as fulfilling basic entry requirements by all the universities of the member states. The success of this educational experiment encouraged the European Economic Community (and the European Atomic Energy Commission), both of which were eventually taken over by the executive institutions of the EEC, to persuade the authorities to establish other European schools at their various centres of government.

At the time of writing there are fourteen European schools in seven different countries (see Table 1.1).

In addition, there are twelve accredited Category II and III European schools with more at the planning stage.

The European Schools Network has its own rules in terms of enrolment, funding and management, as well as its own curriculum. The system was first created as an instrument to meet the educational needs of the children of the civil servants working in Luxembourg for the then

Table 1.1 Category I European Schools

School	Member state	Creation	First Baccalaureate
Luxembourg I	Luxembourg	1953	1959
Brussels I	Belgium	1958	1964
Mol/Geel	Belgium	1960	1966
Varese	Italy	1960	1965
Karlsruhe	Germany	1962	1968
Bergen	The Netherlands	1963	1971
Brussels II	Belgium	1974	1982
Munich	Germany	1977	1984
Culham	United Kingdom	1978	1982
Brussels III	Belgium	1999	2001
Alicante	Spain	2002	2006
Frankfurt	Germany	2002	2006
Luxembourg II	Luxembourg	2004	2013
Brussels IV	Belgium	2007	2017

Source: Office of the Secretary General of the European Schools (2017)

newly formed European Union. The different stakeholders, i.e. parents, institution officials, civil servants and policy-makers, reached an agreement that these children should have the opportunity to be educated in their mother tongue, as well as having the same standard of education as their national classmates in their home countries. Two-thirds of the funding comes from the institutions of the European Union.

The system has remained almost unchanged for nearly six decades, maintaining an enrolment policy that gives priority to children of European Union civil servants. Moreover, from the outset the system has offered its own school certificate, the European Baccalaureate, which is recognised in law by all the universities in the European Union (cf. Office of the Secretary General of the European Schools 2017). In 2009 the system undertook its most significant reforms to date, although the genesis of these reforms goes further back. The reforms focused on three areas: opening up the system and the European Baccalaureate to other students, governing arrangements in the system, and cost-sharing amongst the member states.

'Opening up' is the appellation that the Board of Governors has used in all the official documentation relating to the first element of the 2009 reforms of the European schools. This refers to the development of an accreditation procedure for the creation of additional European schools. The accredited national schools are classified as European schools Category II or III, while traditional European schools are classified as Category I. The principal difference between these three types of European schools is that Category II and III schools do not recruit exclusively the children of civil servants, but have been established to spread European schooling to the general population in Europe. The system of governance as well as the system of funding in Category II and III schools also differs from traditional Category I European schools. The principal difference between Category II and III schools is that a Category II European school receives a proportional subsidy from the EU in relation to the number of children of civil servants attending it. Category II pupils are admitted through a financial agreement between the schools and a number of accredited organisations and companies. In contrast, Category III European schools are in no way dependent on European institutions, except in so far as the Board of Governors forges an agreement with the school to certify that the establishment offers European schooling. The distinction between Category II and Category III schools has become less important recently. Category III schools are now referred to as accredited schools.

Category I pupils are in the main children of officials and contract staff (in post for at least one year) of the EU institutions and of the staff of the European schools, and of the European Patent Office in the case of the Munich school. The percentage of pupils belonging to Category I has been steadily increasing in recent years and this category now accounts for 79.8% of the pupil population (September 2016). The Brussels and Luxembourg schools, where there are large numbers of EU officials and a lack of school places requires a restrictive enrolment policy to be enforced for Category II and III pupils, have a high percentage of Category I pupils, over 90% in the four Brussels schools (100% for Berkendael); whereas the schools located in places where the number of EU officials is small have a far lower percentage of such pupils. A new school in Brussels has just been commissioned. Category II pupils account for 4% of the pupil population, and Category III pupils constitute 16.1% of the total population. (These figures are as of September 2016.)

The second element of the policy of opening up involves the transformation of the European Baccalaureate. Category II and Category III schools were allowed to offer the same final certificate as Category I European schools. The Baccalaureate is legally recognised in all European universities. Both the system of accredited schools and the process of widening access to the European Baccalaureate are underpinned by the idea that the whole system shares a common pedagogical ethos. We examine the usefulness and sustainability of the examination arrangements made within the system, and point to the conflicting and at times contradictory purposes, learning and accreditation, of the European Baccalaureate in Chap. 5.

This broadening and expanding is based on the idea that the notion of European schooling is a particular, exportable and replicable type of education. This principle is currently operationalised through a centralised system that gives the Board of Governors control over setting, correcting and adapting the common criteria of evaluation. Such criteria were established in 2005 and have been updated periodically. Jacques Delors, the former president of the European Commission, once called the European schools 'a sociological and pedagogical laboratory' (Delors 1993). Indeed, the most common adjectives used in the literature to refer to European schools are those of pioneering and experimental.

The second element of the 2009 reforms allowed the granting of more autonomy to Category I schools. This autonomy, referring as it does to pedagogical, administrative and financial arrangements, was designed to allow decisions that can reasonably be taken at school level to be made there, that is, the most immediate level that is consistent with their resolution. This is the principle of subsidiarity and in this context it covers matters such as in-service training, staff development, the use of information and communication technologies, data protection, child protection, transfers provided by the financial regulations and enrolments of pupils. The third element of the reforms referred to new arrangements relating to cost sharing amongst the member states, and in particular, to the costs of the secondment of teachers.

Different writers who have examined the European Schools, such as Shore and Finaldi (2005) and Savvides (2006a, b, c), agree that one of the principal limits of the system is its selective nature. In 2007 the European Parliament requested an extensive analysis of the academic and professional careers of the European schools' graduates and their backgrounds (European Commission 2007a, b). This showed, amongst other findings and unsurprisingly, that some of the traditional European Schools recruited more than 90% of their student population from the same family background, i.e. European civil servants. In the case of the European schools located in Brussels and Luxembourg the demand from Category I children is higher than the number of places available.

One of the reasons for the exclusive character of the schools is that they subscribe to a particular mission and function. The regulations of the system affirm that 'the setting-up of a European School is [...] justified only when it is vital to ensure the optimum operation of an essential Community [European Union] activity' (Board of Governors 2009: 4). In this sense the criteria for opening new schools are not easily met, and the final decision always depends on the willingness of the member states to initiate the process. Throughout the years there have been many cases where these conditions have been met and yet new schools have not been opened, particularly in cities other than Brussels and Luxembourg. The decision to open a new school remains a political decision. The power to establish new European schools is a formal and exclusive competence that only the member states and their national governments have. In other words, the European institutions and the management bodies of the European schools do not have the capacity to open up and extend the system: 'the proposal that a European School be set up on the territory of a Member State is initiated by the State in question' (Board of Governors 2009: 4).

The special character of the schools does not reside exclusively in their European identity, but principally in the fact that they are offering an education based on schooling elements that do not exist at the national levels, such as: early multilingual schooling, a unified curriculum across Europe, a pedagogy based on a pluralistic national perspective, and a multinational student environment. The System's intention is to foster such particularities at the same time as encouraging a sense of European awareness, promoting knowledge about the institutions, their history and a developing sense of citizenship at the European level.

The language policy of the schools has occasioned the most scrutiny (cf. Baetens Beardsmore 1993; Bulmer 1990). European schools are organised in language sections. Students generally speaking receive their education in their native language. The study of a first foreign language (English, French or German), known as L2, is compulsory in each school, from the first year of primary school. In addition, all students must study a second foreign language (L3) from the first year of secondary school. Significantly, the subjects of history, geography and economics (the latter from the fourth year onwards) are studied in the student's first foreign language from the third year of secondary school, instead of in their mother tongue.

The second area of interest has focused on analysing the history and general functioning of the schools (cf. Swan 1996; Shore and Finaldi 2005; Smith 1995). In addition, there are a small number of recent studies that are beginning to offer new lines of investigation, in particular in relation to the study of the European dimension of the system (cf. Savvides 2006a, b, c). We examine this European dimension in more detail in Chap. 4.

The Category 1 European schools are located in those cities where the European Union has deployed its main administrative bodies. Brussels and Luxembourg have 6 of the 14 Category I European schools, accounting for more than 60% of the total student population. In order to set up a Category 1 European school, the Board of Governors approved in 2000 the indicative document containing the *Critères pour l'ouverture, la fermeture ou le maintien des Écoles Européennes* (Board of Governors 2000). Best known in the system by the name of the rapporteur, the *Gaignage* criteria set a number of conditions that justify politically the creation of a Category 1 European school. The experience since 2000 is that these criteria are not easily met in cities other than Brussels and Luxembourg. For the opening of a Category 1 European school the document mandates that the Board of Governors must take into account three elements: a minimum number of language sections; a minimum number of students per language section; and a minimum number of Category I students. In addition, the initiative for opening a new Category 1 European school has to come from the member state where the school is to be located.

Language

European schools have to deal with a paradoxical situation. On the one hand the founding principle of the System calls for the establishment of language sections corresponding to the linguistic background of their students. On the other, the *Gaignage* criteria of 2000 state that there has to be a minimum number of students from the same language background before a corresponding section can be created (Board of Governors 2000). The four European schools in Brussels are examples of schools that have sought to maintain a level of diversity and coherence with their intakes. Consequently, the number of SWALS (Students without a Language Section) has steadily increased since 2007 and for the year 2011–2012 the number rose to 676, representing approximately 7% of the total population of the European schools in Brussels (Board of Governors 2011). Since then the number of SWALS shows no signs of decreasing.

Not all European schools offer the same types of language section. A Lithuanian student, for example, will have a restricted choice in Brussels.

The only school with a Lithuanian section is Brussels II. In some European schools, and for some languages, due to a lack of available students it has not been possible to create specific language sections. The main issue regarding language arrangements in the Category 1 European schools is maintaining a high degree of plurality and diversity of their language sections, while at the same time fulfilling the indicative criteria set by the Gaignage Report in 2000.

Language is the factor that best explains the genesis and evolution of the system. The schools were founded with a particular and specific purpose in mind. Civil servants arriving in Luxembourg in 1953 wanted their children to retain their own cultural heritage. This was achieved by creating a system where the different children could learn in their mother tongue following the same standards as in their country of origin. In that sense the history of the system shows that the principle that governs European schools is language pluralism, not assimilation.

Three *langues véhiculaires* have a special status: French, German and English. Students have to choose between one of these when they enter the first year of the primary school, and they will keep their langue véhiculaire (L2) until the Baccalaureate. The L2 will not only be a language course, it will become the second working language of each student, since it is compulsory that students attend history and geography classes in the L2 they choose on entry, plus economics from S4 (the fourth level of secondary education) if chosen as an option and, since September 2014, religion or ethics from S3 (the third level of secondary education).

The status of these working languages is a source of academic debate. Swan (1996), for example, suggested over twenty years ago that other European countries such as France, Britain and Germany already have their own network of schools abroad, which offer their children an alternative, if often expensive, source of education where their own native language is the language of instruction. However, some of the smaller member states do not provide such an alternative. Swan's argument consists of defending the idea that the languages that are getting most benefit from the language policy of European schools are precisely the ones that are not véhiculaires. Indeed, the fact that European schools aim to offer language sections in all the languages spoken throughout the European Union, though this can only be realised by a cluster of schools, offers the chance to the parents coming from all the member states to enrol their children in their language section, without depending on the setting up of a Polish school or a Spanish school in Brussels. Yet, the offer in terms of diversity is much more limited in practice. None of the European schools include all the language sections for all the official languages of the European Union.

This has created the need to integrate those students who do not have their own language section. Students Without a Language Section (SWALS) have to attend one of the language sections available, while receiving a separate programme in their mother tongue. At primary and secondary levels they only receive one class in their native language, the rest of the courses being taught in the language of the section into which they have chosen to integrate. SWALS are normally enrolled in one of the working language sections. This then becomes their L2. They can also be enrolled in their host country language section, on the condition that no additional costs are involved. Since 2011 Category III pupils have been enrolled with their L1 being the language of their section.

Shore and Finaldi (2005) have also argued in favour of the language policy of the schools. In their study, they suggest that although officially portrayed as a matter of language development, the most noteworthy aspect of this language policy is that the teacher will hardly ever share the same nationality with his or her students. At the heart of this practice seems to be an explicit attempt to separate nationality from the teaching of sensitive subjects such as history or geography. SWALS are only ever taught their L1 by a teacher from their own country. Increasingly, students are taught by teachers from a range of nationalities, as more subjects are taught in L2 and because more non-native teachers have been recruited. Generally however, it should be recalled that the first principle of the European schools is primacy of mother tongue teaching and the system is built round the secondment of teachers from national systems so that in most sections (certainly the non-véhiculaire sections), teachers of core subjects do share the same nationality as their students. Table 1.2 gives an indication of the nationality of the population of students in 2016.

Swan (1996) also looked at the use of the langues véhiculaires as an integral part of the curriculum. He suggested that teaching history to students with other nationalities has the advantage that it provides an

Table 1.2 Pupil population by nationality and by national populations

Nationality	Population 2015–2016 (National population – 1st July 2016)	%
Austrian	354 (8,569,633)	1.3
Belgian	2737.25 (11,371,928)	10.3
British	1314.67 (65,111,143)	4.9
Bulgarian	442.83 (7,097,796)	1.7
Croatian	121.17 (4,225,001)	0.5
Cypriot, inc. North Cypriot	52.17 (1,176,598)	0.2
Czech	431 (10,548,058)	1.6
Danish	531.5 (5,690,750)	2.0
Dutch	920.67 (16,979,729)	3.4
Estonian	264 (1,309,104)	1.0
Finnish	554.42 (5,523,904)	2.1
French	3222.08 (64,668,129)	12.1
German	3358.17 (80,682,351)	12.6
Greek	989.83 (10,919,459)	3.7
Hungarian	515.08 (9,821,318)	1.9
Irish	452.5 (4,713,993)	1.7
Italian	2650.75 (59,801,004)	9.9
Latvian	270.33 (1,955,742)	1.0
Lithuanian	372.17 (2,850,030)	1.4
Luxembourg	241.25 (576,243)	0.9
Maltese	74.75 (419,615)	0.3
Polish	800.92 (38,593,161)	3.0
Portuguese	684 (10,304,434)	2.6
Romanian	488.17 (19,372,734)	1.8
Slovakian	323 (5,429,418)	1.2
Slovenian	210.33 (2,069,362)	0.8
Spanish	2275.58 (46,064,604)	8.5
Swedish	607.17 (9,851,852)	2.3
Others	1431.25	5.4
Total	26,691	100

Source: Office of the Secretary General of the European Schools (2017)
Note: The figures in this table are not 'round numbers'. A large number of pupils enrolled in the European Schools have more than one nationality. Pupils with dual nationality or more are calculated as shares: dual nationality as 0.5 + 0.5, triple nationality as 0.33 + 0.33 + 0.33.

opportunity to question attitudes held by people in schools, at home or in international schools dominated by the language and culture of that particular country. Yet, when examining the textbooks used in European schools this need to develop a European sensitivity is more a matter for the teacher than the tools available. Textbooks are the same ones that are used in national systems. In that sense it is up to the teachers to develop a specific transnational approach when teaching history and geography, and that it is not just a question of teaching national history in a European context or incorporating historical narratives from all the European Union countries into the syllabus. It is also a matter of developing a genuine multilingual, pluricultural and hermeneutic view of history and history teaching.

Finaldi-Baratieri (2005) points out that the principle of equality of esteem between different languages is more difficult to achieve in practical than in theoretical terms. In her view, the policy of langues véhiculaires illustrates how European schools can be more nationalistic than the official discourse would allow. More interestingly, she argues that the working language policy testifies to, at the micro-level, the force and power exerted by the European Union's core member states. Indeed, the system is imperfect when implementing the policy of equality of esteem between languages. Behind the plurality offered, the reality is much more constrained and limited. And yet, despite the imperfect translation into practice of this theoretical principle as the basis of the multilingual policy of the schools, the educational offer in terms of language diversity remains higher than the offer in the rest of the educational systems in Europe. Despite these problems, the language policy still illustrates something unique: the political will to expand the system to all European languages. We examine in Chap. 3 and in much greater detail the organisation of language learning and the development of intercultural competence in the European School System.

Admission and Access

Table 1.3 shows the number of pupils for each school and the total numbers registered in the system for the period 2013–2016 and the variation between years. The number of pupils at Brussels 1 is supplemented by

Table 1.3 Pupil population from 2013 to 2016

School	Pop. 2013	% 2013	Pop. 2014	% 2014	Pop. 2015	% 2015	Pop. 2016	% 2016	Diff. 2013–16 Pop.	Diff. 2013–16%
Alicante	1042	−1.0	1007	−3.4	980	−2.7	1010	3.1	−32	−3.1
Bergen	565	1.6	552	−2.3	537	−2.7	526	−2.0	−39	−6.9
Brussels 1	3083	1.4	3278	6.3	3394	3.5	3344	−1.5	261	8.5
Berkendael							154		154	
Brussels 2	3078	−2.1	2958	−3.9	2998	1.4	3056	1.9	−22	−0.7
Brussels 3	2870	−0.8	2906	1.3	2989	2.9	3041	1.7	171	6.0
Brussels 4	1932	26.3	2263	17.1	2498	10.4	2703	8.2	771	39.9
Culham	600	−12	537	−10.5	459	−14.5	390	−15.0	−210	−35.0
Frankfurt	1247	4.7	1424	14.2	1452	2.0	1465	0.9	218	17.5
Karlsruhe	925	1.5	863	−6.7	813	−5.8	837	3.0	−88	−9.5
Luxembourg1	2786	2.6	2972	6.7	3081	3.7	3260	5.8	474	17.0
Luxembourg2	2101	6.9	2243	6.8	2348	4.7	2531	7.8	430	20.5
Mol	738	−0.8	723	−2.0	722	−0.1	740	2.5	2	0.3
Munich	2183	5.8	2237	2.5	2261	1.1	2313	2.3	130	6.0
Varese	1397	0.9	1422	1.8	1371	−3.6	1321	−3.6	−76	−5.4
Total	24,547	2.8	25,385	3.4	25,903	2.0	26,691	3.0	2144	8.7

Source: Office of the Secretary General of the European Schools (2017)

those pupils located at the Berkendael site, as an extension of the main campus. This relocation is temporary, pending the opening of Brussels 5. These figures do not include associate schools.

The total student population of the European schools (October 2016) was 26,691, and this represents a 3% growth in comparison with the previous year. 67.7% of the total student population goes to one or other of the four Brussels schools (46%) (at the time of writing a new school in Brussels is being opened) and the two Luxembourg schools (21.7%). The European schools located in Brussels have systematically suffered from a problem of overcrowding for the past ten years.

When faced with the problem of scarcity of places, the Board of Governors has been applying in the last six years a restrictive enrolment policy for Category III students. As indicated in the official enrolment policy for 2013–2014, the enrolment of such students is 'restrict[ed] to the siblings of present students, abiding strictly by the decisions of the Board of Governors concerning this category of pupils' (Board of Governors 2012: 3). This has led to a decrease in the percentage of Category III children in the European schools in Brussels, providing new arguments for the debate about the potential homogeneity of students within the schools. The difficulty with solving the problem of, for example, overcrowding in Brussels, is leading to a major issue of legitimacy. The reforms of 2009 were implemented to 'open up' the system to other children than those in Category I, though accredited schools had been introduced earlier. While the System has started to open up outside the Belgian capital, in the Category 1 European schools the issue relating to the legitimacy of the whole system of admissions has become more acute, and has only been partly solved by the opening of a new school in Brussels.

Schooling

In 2006 the Board of Governors decided to commission an independent analysis of four of the smaller Category 1 European schools located across Europe. The outcome was the report submitted by the Bureau van Dijk Management Consultants SA in August 2006 (Van Dijk 2006). This report included a brief comparative analysis of the European schools and the potential alternatives in terms of international schooling in the four cities studied.

The team of consultants based their conclusions on a series of interviews with the parents, teachers and directors of these four European schools. The Report stated that among the most praised features of the system was that 'comparatively speaking international schools do not offer language tuition as diversified and as intensive as European schools' (ibid.: 13). Two other elements were highly praised by parents: the first of these was the European Baccalaureate, which is 'recognized by nearly all the Member States and therefore allows their children to follow their studies in any European universities' (ibid.: 13); and the second was 'the multicultural and European citizen spirit brought by the multilingual education of European schools, these being certainly not perceivable in the international schools' (ibid.: 14).

This is a home grown system that is sixty years old, and based on a model of an elite European education long superseded by changes in society as well as the Commission itself (not least the growth of the European Union from the original six countries in 1952 to the current twenty-eight countries, though the United Kingdom is at the time of writing seeking to leave the European Union). It is widely agreed that the current system shows signs of inconsistency across different schools and language sections, and that it also shows signs of incoherence. Many students leave the system at ages between 14 and 16 (secondary years S4 and S5) when it is reported that the science curriculum, for example, becomes significantly more difficult. There is meant to be a free choice of options for students, but the reality is closer to a fairly loose assemblage of available subjects and options that changes from school to school and from year to year. There is an overemphasis on timetabling allocation of subjects as a proxy for quality and academic difficulty.

Some teaching groups are extremely small due to a number of factors based on taken for granted assumptions about pedagogy that may not be valid. Within the system, parents' perceptions of student identity are very important, as well as the ability to transfer to university. There is some confusion around the role of languages within the system, and a lack of consideration given to issues surrounding non-modern foreign language subjects in second and third languages, particularly with regards to the needs of the smaller language sections. There are problems with the European Baccalaureate as a qualification, particularly relating to the use of oral examinations, marking systems, conversion tables and quality assurance systems.

The European schools language policy is embodied above all: in the principle of supporting L1 learning through the creation of language sections; in the provision of additional support for students without a language section; in having students study content subjects through their L2; and by offering L3, L4 and L5 language courses. However, there is no overarching language policy document that guides the co-construction of learning environments that foster bilingualism, trilingualism or multilingualism, though a vision on the use of language is expressed in the Founding Convention and also in the Principles of the European Schools (cf. Office of the Secretary General of the European Schools 2017).

Changing the System

We also need to make sense of the notion of change or alteration. Objects and relations between objects, educational systems and people change their form over time. An example of this change process at the epistemological level is the invention (insofar as the set of concepts and relations between them is new) of the notion of probability (cf. Hacking 2005) in the nineteenth century, and this changed the way social objects could be conceived and ultimately arranged. Change can occur in four ways: contingent ontological, planned ontological, epistemically-driven ontological, and in the transitive realm of knowledge, epistemological (cf. Scott 2011). With regards to the example above, the invention of probability, two phases of change can be identified. The first is where knowledge is created and thus operates at the epistemological level, the new arrangement of knowledge. The second is where this knowledge has real effects at the ontological level, so that new arrangements, new formations, new assemblages come into being. The dilemma is that the social world, in contrast to the physical world, is always in a state of transition and flux, so that it is hard to argue that there are invariant laws by which the world works, at all times and in all places, except in a basic logical and rational sense.

Societies are characterised by notions of continuous emergence, flux and change. Objects in the world cannot be characterised by their essential qualities, but only through their interactions with other objects. Complexity resides in all these various interactions which produce new objects (understood as different forms of structure), and results in a bewildering array of arrangements of material and human objects; and because they are difficult to characterise rarely allow definitive accounts of what is going on to be produced. It is the complexity of these object-interactions and their subsequent and temporary coalescences that makes it difficult to provide complete descriptions of them. The epistemological level is unsynchronised with the ontological level because researchers and investigators have not developed sufficiently their instruments and conceptual schema for capturing something that is both ever-changing and has too many elements to it, i.e. it is too complex. However, this doesn't categorically rule out the possibility of providing more complete descriptions of events, structures, mechanisms and their relations in the world, and this suggests a notion of human fallibility which means that human actions are corrigible. The twin elements of complexity and temporal emergence cannot preclude correct descriptions being made of activities in the world, only that these elements can create considerable difficulties. This is further compounded by how emergence operates in the world.

Many theorists go further than this (for example, Osberg and Biesta 2007), and hold to a version of emergence in which there is a radical incommensurability between different formations over time (whether material, embodied or discursive). Furthermore, it is impossible to predict what inter-connections, new formations, and iterations of the object-system will be realised because the principles of the new mechanism are not given in the current arrangements. In other words, the relations between objects and the objects themselves, which make up activity systems, are not patterned in any meaningful sense; there is a radical incommensurability between these different iterations.

All discussions of a person or an education system over time require some understanding of change; that is, the notion of change is built into the conception of the human being or system. There is also the problem of persistence. If there was no cohering element between time moments, so that every moment entails a change of person or system, we would not have a sense of personhood or system identity, which therefore has to include a notion of persistence over time, and, in addition, has a notion of emergence. And this is emergence understood in its two modes: as a temporal phenomenon and ontologically as a response to the stratified nature of reality.

Insight into problems faced by an education system and awareness of potential solutions do not necessarily lead to the ability to act in an effective manner in order to guide stakeholders in instituting a change. The rapid and successful implementation of reforms in a school system is directly dependent on the quality of the knowledge, skills and thinking that a system and those that introduce its planned reforms bring to the reform process. Moreover, innovations and reforms call for new and often substantially improved, knowledge, skills and thinking in several domains. This includes knowledge about obstacles to change at both the instrumental and affective levels and about the change process itself.

Michael Fullan (2001) suggests a number of strategies for reforming an education system: maintaining a focus on moral purpose; understanding the change process; increasing coherence among various aspects of a planned change; relationship-building; knowledge creation and sharing; and building commitment among an organisation's internal and external members (stakeholders). Fullan focuses on consciously being aware of, shaping and using the ideational realm of aspirations, commitments and values, as well as on the mechanics of how people work together, create and manage knowledge.

However, despite what is known about educational change, it is noteworthy that education systems and their 'institutional arrangements are stubbornly resistant to change'. Argyris (2010) goes even further arguing that organisations and their leaders tend to be trapped in the status quo and in their own behaviours. These behaviours are often characterised by a tendency to blame others, and self-deception and rationalisations. Similarly, Kegan and Lahey (2009) identify a common malaise of immunity to change at both the individual and institutional levels. Two central messages about overcoming resistance to change rise out of the work of leading thinkers in change management. The first is that those leading change require high levels of meta-cognitive, meta-affective and meta-social awareness. The second is that people arrive at work with their personal understandings and feelings, and that these need to be explored in relation to work in order to understand their impact on the work process. In other words, change in the workplace almost always requires more than mechanical or technical solutions. Whatever changes are sought, usually these also need to lead to a change in beliefs, feelings, knowledge and behaviours, if this change is to be sustainable.

To move beyond purely mechanistic solutions, Kegan and Lahey (2009) argue that this requires the identification of those assumptions that are driving decision-making. Assumptions are something we take as being true without thorough investigation. For example, if a stated organisational commitment is to distribute leadership in order to ultimately improve student learning, a leader may still not delegate sufficiently because he or she does not wish to lose control. He or she may believe that holding onto control is a way of maintaining standards. Until that underlying assumption is challenged through analysis, and the development of a belief in the capacity of others to lead, substantial change will not take place. Kegan and Lahey (ibid.) propose that individuals need to be supported in exploring their own individual immunity to planned changes, and that the institution needs to explore its collective immunity to the desired or planned change. Without challenging underlying assumptions at both the personal and institutional level, it will be difficult for an organisation to institute change.

One of the most important change mechanisms is political and we will examine this type of mechanism in greater detail in the chapters that follow: the curriculum in Chap. 2; the role of languages in the system in Chap. 3; European nationalism and schooling in Chap. 4; assessment reforms of the system in Chap. 5; external relations with other systems of education such as the various European higher education systems in Chap. 6; and, most importantly, cosmopolitan and European conceptualisations of schooling in the last chapter.

A team of researchers from UCL Institute of Education, a constituent college of the University of London, which included the authors of this book, carried out the research for this project during the academic year 2014–2015, as part of a European Commission funded evaluation project looking specifically at the upper secondary phase of education in the European Schools System. During this time we spoke to representatives of all the stakeholder groups, including students, teachers and parents, as well as key senior figures in the Office of the Secretary General, and the European Commission. We also visited different European Schools and sat in on meetings. We carried out significant amounts of desk research, and reviewed internal documents (cf. Leaton Gray et al. 2015). In the next chapter, we examine the curriculum of the European Schools and how this has changed during the life history of the system.

Open Access This chapter is licensed under the terms of the Creative Commons Attribution 4.0 International License (http://creativecommons.org/licenses/by/4.0/), which permits use, sharing, adaptation, distribution and reproduction in any medium or format, as long as you give appropriate credit to the original author(s) and the source, provide a link to the Creative Commons license and indicate if changes were made.

The images or other third party material in this chapter are included in the chapter's Creative Commons license, unless indicated otherwise in a credit line to the material. If material is not included in the chapter's Creative Commons license and your intended use is not permitted by statutory regulation or exceeds the permitted use, you will need to obtain permission directly from the copyright holder.

2

Acquainted with All that Is Great and Good: Designing a Twenty-First Century Curriculum

Governments round the world and coordinators and curriculum developers of systems of education such as the European School System at the end of the twentieth century and in the early part of the twenty-first century, with a few notable exceptions, have reached an agreement about the nature of the school curriculum, learning approaches and assessment practices. This consensus now operates at all levels of education systems, and can be expressed in terms of a number of propositions: traditional knowledge forms and strong insulations between them need to be preserved; each of these knowledge forms can be expressed in terms of lower and higher level domains and the latter have to be taught before the former and sequenced correctly; certain groups of children are better able to access the curriculum than other children, and, as a result, a differentiated curriculum is necessary to meet the needs of all school learners; the teacher's role is to impart this body of knowledge in the most effective way, and thus their brief cannot concern itself with the ends to which education is directed, but only the means for its efficient delivery; and the school's role is to deliver a public service that meets the targets set for it by governments and other such educational systems.

The most important element of the European School System is its curriculum, and therefore we need in the first instance to understand what a

© The Author(s) 2018
S. Leaton Gray et al., *Curriculum Reform in the European Schools*,
https://doi.org/10.1007/978-3-319-71464-6_2

curriculum is. A curriculum points to what is intended should happen in a programme of learning and the circumstances in which these activities can take place. Those activities are learning activities; and thus a curriculum is a collection of exercises and tasks, which culminate in learning of one type or another. There are three types of learning: cognitive, skill-based and dispositional, and they have different forms and operate in different ways. Cognition is the manipulation of those symbolic resources (words, numbers, pictures etc.) that points to something outside itself. Skill-based knowledge is procedural and not declarative; and dispositional knowledge refers to relatively stable habits of mind and body, sensitivities to occasion and participation repertoires. Significantly, these three types of learning are focused on knowledge-construction and are knowledge-development activities, although there are some important differences between the three types. And what can be inferred from this is that how knowledge is construed will determine how appropriate learning environments are constructed and ultimately how learners then learn in and from them.

The learning aims and objectives of a curriculum do not specify how the knowledge, skills, and dispositions should be taught, though teaching and learning approaches are derived from them. As a consequence the curriculum-developer needs to reconceptualise each intended learning outcome into a programme of learning or action learning set. Pedagogic approaches and strategies range from didactic to imitative to reflective and meta-reflective action learning sets, and they have a number of common characteristics. A pedagogic approach specifies: the circumstances in which it can be used in the learning environment; the resources and technologies which allow that learning to take place; the type of relationship between teacher and learner, and learner and learner, to effect that learning; a theory of learning, or, in other words, a theory of how that construct (i.e. knowledge set, skill or disposition) can be assimilated; and a theory of transfer held by the teacher, that is, how the learning which has taken place in a particular set of circumstances (i.e. a classroom, with a set of learners, in a particular way, with a particular theory of learning underpinning it, and so forth) can transfer to other environments in other places and times. Paying due attention to these allows a proper focus on learning, with these being generally neglected in the various iterations of the curriculum in the European School System (both those proposed and those implemented).

Pedagogic arrangements also need to fit with the view of knowledge held by the curriculum-developer. To this end, curriculum decisions need to be made about: pedagogic approaches and strategies (i.e. observation; coaching; goal-orientated learning; mentoring; peer-learning; simulation; instruction; concept-formation; reflection; meta-cognitive learning; problem-solving and practice); relations between knowledge domains (i.e. traditional/fragmented or networked/fully integrated modes); knowledge, skill or dispositional orientations; knowledge framings; progression and pacing; types of relations between teachers and students; relations between types of learners; spatial and temporal arrangements for learning; formative assessment and feedback processes; and the criteria that can be used for evaluating learning. All these need to be taken into account in translating curriculum knowledge into pedagogic knowledge.

Learning aims, objectives and prescriptions, or curriculum standards (i.e. learning objects), are therefore distinguished from these pedagogic approaches and also from assessment arrangements. Frequently, an assessment procedure specifies those knowledge-sets, skills or dispositions that a learner is required to have, and which are expressed in such a way that they can be tested in a controlled environment, such as an examination. The principal problem with assessment procedures of this type is that testing a person's knowledge, skills and dispositions is likely to have washback effects on the original set. Instead of the assessment process acting merely as a descriptive device, it also acts in a variety of ways to transform the curriculum it is seeking to measure. Washback effects work on a range of objects and in different ways. So, for example, there are washback effects on the curriculum, on teaching and learning, on the capacity of the individual and more fundamentally on the structures of knowledge, though these four mechanisms are frequently conflated in the minds of educational stakeholders. Micro washback effects work directly on the person, whereas macro washback effects work directly on institutions and systems, which then subsequently have an impact on individuals within those institutions and systems. Finally, a learner may have to reframe their knowledge or skill set to fit the test, and therefore the assessment of their mastery of this knowledge or skill is not a determination of their competence, but of whether they have successfully understood how to rework their capacity to fit the demands of the examination technology. As a result teaching to the test occurs and the curriculum is narrowed to accommodate those learning outcomes that can more easily be assessed. There is some evidence of this occurring in the European Baccalaureate.

The reason for separating out learning approaches from assessment approaches is now clear. If these assessment approaches are the same as learning approaches, then this is likely to have a detrimental and reductionist effect on the curriculum and more importantly on the type and content of learning that takes place. However, there are different needs within a system of education, and one of these is that, at set points in time, supra-national (such as the European Commission), national and local educational bodies need to have information about how well the system is doing. This is a very different process from improving learning with an individual learner. However, there must be some connecting link between learning and reporting, so that the latter doesn't distort the former, and this is the role of learning aims and objectives.

Learning and assessment practices on a programme of study, such as a curriculum, can be regarded as formative if evidence of a learner's achievements in relation to knowledge and skill acquisition is collected and used by the teacher, the individual student, and their fellow students, with the specific intention of deciding on their subsequent programme of learning. As a result, assessment is used formatively when it directly influences the learner's cognition. Curriculum developers consequently need to make a clear distinction between summative and formative assessment. If these two functions are combined, then the potential impact of the curriculum is weakened.

There are two principles which structure the choice and order of content within a curriculum: a spiral element or a re-visiting of concepts, skills or dispositions at a higher level of intensity and at a later point in the programme of study, and theory transfer from theory to practice and from sites of learning to sites of application. The first of these is the need to incorporate a spiral element into the curriculum, i.e. a set of ideas or operations, once introduced, is revisited and reconstructed in a more formal or operational way, at different stages in the learning programme (cf.

Bruner 1996). And the second refers to the relationships between experience, theory- or concept-development (in the three different domains of knowledge, skill and disposition), strategies for the application of this theory or set of concepts, applications of these learning and practice skills, strategies and plans for action, and evaluations of these practices for the purpose of changing them. The effect is to move the learner into the centre of the practice and away from the periphery.

In order for learning to take place, i.e. increased levels of knowledge, enhanced skill levels and dispositional improvements, the following are important considerations: a minimisation of washback effects; an emphasis on curriculum, rather than assessment-driven change; the preservation of the curriculum as the principal driver of the learning programme rather than that which can be most easily assessed; a clear separation of the evaluative and learning functions in any educational programme; and an intelligible set of curriculum specifications, expressed as learning standards or objects. Though the European School System is better than most other systems in mitigating these harmful effects, there are regressive elements relating to these matters in the current arrangements.

A further point needs to be made about the construction of a curriculum and this refers to how progression is understood within the domains of knowledge from which it has been derived. (This is disciplinary knowledge.) Many curricula round the world employ progression modes that are extensional in design, where this is understood as an increase in the amount, or range, of an activity, whether knowledge-based, skill-oriented or dispositional. This has the effect of limiting, and distorting, the notion of progression, both between items in a curriculum and in terms of the progress a learner makes within that curriculum.

There are a number of other forms of progression and they need to be incorporated into the design of the curriculum. The first of these is prior condition. In the acquisition of particular knowledge, skill and dispositional elements, there are prerequisites in the learning process. A second is maturational, where this refers to the physical development of the mind of the learner. A third is intensification. Whereas extension refers to the amount or range of progression, intensification or complexity refers to the extent to which a sophisticated understanding has replaced a superficial understanding of a concept. In relation to the knowledge constructs, skills and dispositions implicit within the curriculum, there are four forms of complexity that might signify progression. These are behavioural complexity, symbolic complexity, affective complexity and perceptual complexity. There is also a type of progression, abstracting, which involves moving from a concrete understanding of a concept to a more abstract one. A further type of progression is an increased capacity to articulate, explain or amplify an idea or construct, i.e. the learner retains the ability to deploy the skill, and in addition, they can now articulate, explain or amplify what they are able to do and what they have done. And finally progression can be understood as part of a process, and this refers to the way that the learner interacts with the learning object. An example could be moving from an assisted performance to an independent one. This suggests that curricula as they are presently conceived round the world are deficient if they employ extensional forms of progression exclusively at the expense of a range of other types. These forms of progression are not of the same order; however, they refer to different aspects of the process of learning. There is no category error here. They are linked by their capacity to affect different parts of the learning process, and in particular, where an individual moves from one state of being to another. For example, extensional forms of progression focus on the objects of learning, whereas process forms of progression focus on the learner and the way they can and do respond to these objects.

Over the last fifty years, there has been a move away from traditional/fragmented approaches towards networked approaches in some school curricula. There are implications of adopting either fragmented or networked approaches or taking up positions in between. A fragmented or traditional approach fits better with how universities, teachers, parents and students understand curricular divisions at school level; allows choice between subject options whilst retaining core subjects; better reflects current arrangements; and can be better accommodated within traditional pedagogic structures. A networked approach reduces choice because it implies that all aspects of the curriculum have to be covered in the teaching and learning arrangements that are put in place; and may better reflect the nature of subject knowledge. The key question is how to balance these imperatives when undertaking a reform of secondary education in a system such as the one we are focusing on in this book. Thus, there are significant implications of some of these ideas for the curriculum of the European School System, for the constitution of the European Schools Baccalaureate and in particular, for the Baccalaureate rules. There are also implications for higher education access from these schools to European universities.

The European Schools Curriculum

Both the system of European schools and the process of widening access to the European Baccalaureate with regards to three categories of schools are built on the idea that the whole system shares a common pedagogical ethos. The 'opening up' that we referred to earlier is based on the idea that the notion of European schooling is a particular, exportable and replicable type of education. This is currently organised through a centralised system that gives the Board of Governors the authority to set, correct and adapt the common criteria of evaluation. Such criteria were established in 2005 and are updated periodically.

In February 2012 the Joint Teaching Committee, which is the institution with a mandate to oversee all the pedagogical issues of the European Schools System, adopted the following document: 'New Structure for all Syllabuses in the System of the European Schools' (cf. Board of Governors 2012). This document illustrates the path that the European Schools System is taking in terms of pedagogical development. It adopts a common structure for all the syllabuses, and identifies two objectives for the system:

> The European Schools have the two objectives of providing formal education and of encouraging students' personal development in a wider social and cultural context. Formal education involves the acquisition of competences – knowledge, skills and attitudes – across a range of domains. Personal development takes place in a variety of spiritual, moral, social and cultural contexts. (Board of Governors 2012: 3)

Here implicit reference is made to the multicultural environment of the European Schools System:

The students of the European Schools are future citizens of Europe and the world. As such, they need a range of competences if they are to meet the challenges of a rapidly-changing world. In 2006 the European Council and European Parliament adopted a European Framework for Key Competences for Lifelong Learning. It identifies eight key competences which all individuals need for personal fulfilment and development, for active citizenship, for social inclusion and for employment: communication in the mother tongue; communication in foreign languages; mathematical competence and basic competences in science and technology; digital competence; learning to learn; social and civic competences; sense of initiative and entrepreneurship; and cultural awareness and expression. The European Schools' syllabuses seek to develop all of these key competences in the students. (Board of Governors 2012: 3)

Significantly, the pedagogical objectives of the European schools are defined on the basis of the European Framework for Key Competences, as adopted by the European institutions.

The new common structure in terms of pedagogy emphasises the will to connect the European schools with the educational policy of the European Union. The document that emerged from the Joint Teaching Committee makes official the link between the notion of European schooling, as developed by the European schools, and the educational policy of the European Union (cf. Board of Governors 2012), as we can see in the introductory sentence of the document:

> The underlying concept of this structure expresses a change from the contents-oriented syllabus to a competence-based syllabus. The structure of the syllabus is intentionally brief and precise. (Board of Governors 2012: 3)

The tendency to bring closer the pedagogical objectives of the European schools with the European Union is also emphasised in the Alicante Declaration on European Schooling made by Interparents, in April 2012, and in particular in point 14 where parents:

> (a)sk that Member States' determination to invest in the development of quality education, youth and mobility, cultural and linguistic diversity, the European dimension and citizenship as well as a global perspective, Europe 2020-strategy and lifelong learning goals also apply to European Schools. (Board of Governors 2012)

The Alicante declaration identifies directly those issues that are considered to be the bedrock of the educational agenda at the European level: the 2020 strategy and the concept of life-long learning.

The strategy to align the type of pedagogical curriculum offered at the European schools with the educational policies set by the European institutions is also evident in the changes that were introduced to the European Baccalaureate. When the Board of Governors adopted the final report of the working group, *Reform of the European Baccalaureate*, it was agreed that the marking/grading criteria would be inspired by the European Credit Transfer System, which is precisely the marking criterion used by the European Union at the postgraduate level.

The secondary level in European schools comprises seven years. In the first three years all students follow a common course, known as the observation cycle. The majority of the subjects are still taught in the language corresponding to each language section. In the second year of secondary school the learning of a second language, which was already an option at the primary level, is compulsory. In the third year all students take geography and history in the foreign language they have chosen (which is often referred to in the system as the 'working language', or 'langue véhiculaire'). The system offers three working languages (which correspond to the working languages of the European Union): French, English and German.

In secondary years four and five (S4–S5) the compulsory course in science includes physics, chemistry and biology, as well as mathematics. New options are made available from the fourth year, such as economics, a third foreign language and ancient Greek. The last two years, six and seven (S6–S7), form a unit leading to the European Baccalaureate. The compulsory courses include: a national language, L2, mathematics, a science, philosophy, physical education, history and geography. During the years of preparation for the Baccalaureate students choose from a range of options, and they may decide to study some of the compulsory courses as a two period course or at the advanced level as a four period course.

In Geography the principal emphasis is on the European Union. The teachers are also expected to provide historical material for their students relating to the European Union and its institutions, and to discuss the various ways with them in which Europe can be defined, including the natural environment, demography, industry and energy, rural environment, regional policies, etc. The arts and the humanities have a special place in the curriculum, and music is of particular importance. The programme 'has the responsibility for delivering one of the key objectives of the European Schools which is to provide young people with opportunities for creative endeavour and to promote an understanding of a common European heritage' (Board of Governors 2012: 2).

There is a multi-cultural element running through the curriculum. Banks (2007: 139) identifies five dimensions of multicultural education: content integration (using examples and content from a variety of cultures in the teaching); knowledge construction (teachers help students understand the implicit cultural assumptions); prejudice reduction (ethnic, social, economic, nationalist); an empowering school culture; and finally, an equity pedagogy (where teachers modify their teaching in ways that facilitate the academic achievement of students). Of those five dimensions, the European schools prioritise two: content integration and knowledge construction. The curriculum is constructed in order to create an equality of esteem between the different European cultures. This is achieved, for example, by providing transnational examples in the geography or history programmes at the secondary level and by providing at an early age several pedagogical frameworks associated with a common European culture. Furthermore, multilingualism is given a prominent role in the curriculum. Allemann-Ghionda (2012: 126) suggests that 'multilingual education is regarded as a privileged path of intercultural education […], their pedagogies are based on the assumption that acquiring a deep knowledge and an active command of languages other than one's mother tongue has the effect of expanding the mind and enhancing intercultural competence'.

Subjects

Writings about what makes for a good science or mathematics curriculum largely rely on conceptual work and professional wisdom. We lack high quality, large-scale evaluations that rigorously test interventions. For this reason an evidence-based research synthesis (let alone any sort of systematic review) is simply not possible (e.g. Watson et al. 2013, with regards to mathematics). Nevertheless in both science education and mathematics education there is a growing body of evidence-informed work about what makes for a good curriculum. Perhaps the most fundamental issue is that of content. In science education there has been a growing acknowledgement in recent times that many school curricula are overloaded. Too much time is spent covering a myriad of specific, often isolated, pieces of content with the result that the larger picture is lost.

It is clearly important to have a curriculum that facilitates, or at the very least enables, students to progress in their learning as best they can. Studies on students' progression in learning (whether in mathematics, in science or more generally) have often been interpreted as though learning progresses up a ladder or in stages, so that each rung of the ladder (or stage) needs to be reached before subsequent progression can occur. Unsurprisingly, fine-grained observations of students' learning, such as those by Shapiro (1994), reveal that learning is rarely like this. Not only do learners sometimes regress, they also at times miss a stage (or rung on the ladder). The implication for curriculum developers is that concepts need to be ordered in a logical sequence that facilitates learning but it should not be assumed that learning proceeds inflexibly along such a route. Learning can be more like putting together the pieces of a jigsaw, where this can be done successfully in a number of ways rather than in one predetermined order. It is generally agreed in curricula round the world that mathematics and science should be core subjects.

Given this, there are a number of important considerations as to which subjects should be taught in the European Schools' curriculum. Parents and students will invariably bring their own understandings about curriculum planning to any discussion of a reform process. This means that if parents hold traditional views about subjects within a curriculum, for example, that there needs to be three separate sciences (i.e. physics, chemistry and biology), then it follows that, as far as they are concerned, a general science curriculum is going to appear incomprehensible or, in their view, represent a simplification and thus reduction in the quality of this important area of the curriculum. It doesn't matter whether parents are correct in their judgements about the subject make-up of the curriculum, their beliefs are significant factors in any decisions made by European school curriculum-makers, and need to be taken into account accordingly. A system that overrides the views of those closely involved on a day-to-day basis is unhelpful and unresponsive, and any reforms are unlikely to work in practice.

Teachers will also bring their own understandings of curriculum planning to any debate. This has the same effect as with parents, though teachers approach the problem from a different angle. Their perspective emanates from longstanding and perhaps strongly held beliefs about curricular divisions, their own disciplinary perspective (i.e. their university subject and their pedagogical training in that subject) and the syllabuses and curricula they have been teaching for, in some cases, many years. Again, effective reform is impossible without adequate teacher engagement and support, so teachers' views need to be taken seriously.

Specifications for the system from the Board of Governors also play an important part in the debate. These are perhaps best summarised in Article 4 of the Convention:

1. The courses of study shall be undertaken in the languages specified;
2. Certain subjects shall be taught to joint classes of the same level;
3. A particular effort shall be made to give students a thorough knowledge of modern languages;
4. The European dimension shall be developed in the curricula;
5. The conscience and convictions of individuals shall be respected; and
6. Measures shall be taken to facilitate the reception of children with special educational needs.

Article 4 is legally enshrined in the constitution of the European Union.

The European Commission has identified eight key competences for lifelong learning as requirements for underpinning any curriculum reform process. These competences are: communication in the mother tongue; communication in foreign languages; mathematical competence and basic competences in science and technology; digital competence; learning to learn; social and civic competences; a sense of initiative and entrepreneurship; and cultural awareness and expression. In planning any curriculum reform, it is important to avoid subjects that do not have an overall rationale or are not exemplifications of the eight competences;

otherwise the curriculum becomes an arbitrary collection of subjects. Subjects also need to fit with current and/or future arrangements for the Baccalaureate.

A further factor is university entrance. It should be noted that subjects that fall within traditional disciplinary boundaries are also more readily recognised by a range of university systems. However, universities may recognise these subject boundaries as subject divisions at the point of student entry, but arrange knowledge into subjects that do not conform to these traditional subject boundaries, i.e. only a very few universities currently divide their science provision into physics, chemistry and biology. It should also be noted that university entrance requirements can be variable, depending on the national system in operation, the apparent prestige of the university, how competitive course entry needs to be (for example medicine is an example of a highly competitive course), the type of entrance qualification for particular students, overall student numbers, and the length of time a course has been in operation. An important factor in any arrangement of subjects is therefore flexibility. Entry requirements for each of these degrees reflect the subject matter of the degree. The titles of the various degrees do not equate with the titles of the subjects offered currently in the European Schools System. These differences reflect both omissions and particular sets of combinations. They also reflect the type of university or institute of higher education, the various ways those institutions have combined subjects together, their institutional histories, and the availability of teaching staff and other resources. Likewise, the European Schools System's current arrangements reflect the history of the system, the availability of resources (including teacher resources) and the types of schools that have been developed. This means that there is no overall curriculum rationale for the selection of subjects and combinations of subjects in either the European Schools System or the European Higher Education System, though there is some attempt in both to be broad and comprehensive.

However, these differences between the overall European schools' curriculum (in terms of subjects offered) and the overall curriculum of European higher education institutions are not unexpected, and yet, breadth and comprehensiveness are mandated in the European Schools System by the Board of Governors. This is that the curriculum (including choice of subjects, relations between core, option and complementary subjects, length of instructional time given to each of those subjects, etc.) should reflect the eight core competences. Otherwise, decisions relating to choice of subjects, relations between those subjects, the content of those subjects, and the length of instructional time for these subjects become a matter of special pleading and are relatively arbitrary.

Philosophy is an example of this. A number of arguments have been put forward to support the idea that it should be central to the European schools' curriculum. Philosophy already forms a part of the Baccalaureates for France, Italy and Spain. Students applying to universities in these countries without philosophy as a component of their pre-university qualification are placed at a disadvantage. Some European citizens might think of a European Baccalaureate, which didn't include philosophy, as a second-class qualification. Indeed, philosophy provides a foundation for law, psychology, economics, theology, literature, history, geography, etc. and in addition is a coordinating and unifying subject in its own right. And further to this, philosophy is the only subject that allows students to consolidate and unify knowledge across the disciplines. Without philosophy in the curriculum as a compulsory subject, students graduate with fragmented packets of knowledge, and no framework that encompasses all the disciplines and allows them to develop a consistent, intellectual worldview. The philosophy syllabus therefore fills in critical gaps that exist in other parts of the European schools curriculum. For example, the philosophy course is the only place that students study civics, political theory, epistemology, philosophy of science, ethics etc. For many S6 and S7 year students, this helps them to make sense of the academic knowledge that they have acquired and creates a framework for their knowledge. In addition, philosophy fits well into the competency curriculum, being relevant to competences five, six, seven and eight: learning to learn; social and civic competences; sense of initiative and entrepreneurship; and cultural awareness and expression. These are powerful arguments for philosophy being central to the European schools' curriculum, and for being a core rather than optional subject, quite aside from any thoughts about university admissions requirements.

Latin is another example where it is relatively easy to make a strong case for its continued inclusion in the curriculum. A number of arguments have been developed as to why Latin should be a part of the curriculum. Students want to study it and thus limiting or eliminating it would restrict choice and diminish the possibilities for learning implied by offering choice to students, i.e. they are more likely to be motivated in their studies if they have some choice in what they study. Latin is the foundation for many European languages and thus studying Latin facilitates the learning of many of these languages. The language of Latin has cultural significance for European students. For those students who want to study ancient civilizations at European universities, studying Latin is particularly advantageous.

Disagreement about the content areas of the curriculum occurs in all subjects and religious education is no exception. However, controversy about the purpose of the religious education curriculum can be particularly intense. A well-established aim of much religious education is to maintain the faith of students in one particular religion or denomination (i.e. confessional religious education). Such an approach is often popular with certain parents who want to see a school promoting the same religious way of understanding the world that they provide in their homes. This aim is often found in what are typically referred to as faith schools (whether publicly or privately funded), by which is meant that one particular understanding of religious faith predominates. Proponents of this approach may argue that parents have a right to ensure that their children are educated within a particular religious framework or ethos.

As with philosophy, Latin and perhaps religious studies, we can see that a special case can be made for each of them as a core subject, or at least as an optional alternative, in the secondary curriculum. Yet the problem with maintaining student choice at the levels currently permitted, and (for example) maintaining instruction in particular subjects such as philosophy, religious studies or Latin, is that it has led to a very complex and diverse system with inconsistencies between schools. In some cases students are denied their first choices, or required to take subjects that they do not want to take. Currently, at S6 and S7 in the science specialisation, students are obliged to choose at least two options from biology, chemistry, ICT, physics and geography. Mathematics 5 is compulsory for students choosing physics. Human sciences are compulsory for those students not choosing geography.

Curriculum Alternatives

We now sketch out three general alternatives: a curriculum without options, a curriculum with option choices within pathways, and a curriculum offering core and option subjects, and discuss each of these below. The first alternative is to eliminate options and teach elements of all the possible subjects that could be a part of the curriculum (and this would include subjects which currently are not offered in the European schools' curriculum such as psychology, linguistics, sociology, history of art, engineering, etc.) or are recognised as subjects by European universities (see Table 2.1). This could be achieved in a number of ways. General subject areas or pathways (and some of these are recognised in European university curricula) are created along the lines of the mandatory eight European competences, and all the possible subjects and all the subjects recognised by European universities are allocated to these areas. For example, instead of offering history (European or otherwise), geography, religious studies, ancient civilizations, literature, fine art and history of art, music history and appreciation, law, archaeology, architecture and philosophy, elements of these could come under the overall subject heading of humanities or cultural studies. Another example is social studies. So for example, instead of offering psychology, sociology, statistical science, economics, business studies and political science as options, elements of these are subsumed into a generic area of study or pathway, which could be called social studies or social sciences. A third example is natural sciences, and this would incorporate physics, chemistry, biology, biochemistry, biotechnology, technology, earth science, astronomy and medicine. What this effectively means is that weak boundaries are being established in the curriculum between subjects and that a more networked approach to curriculum design is being adopted.

In these three examples, students wouldn't choose between these subject areas, they would study all of them. However, unless more time was allocated to the teaching of the curriculum, this restricts the amount of time given to each of the subject areas (whether this is expressed as number of periods or as number of minutes of study). It delays specialisation of study by the student and effectively locates this decision at the point of entry to higher education. Such a proposal restricts content (defined as knowledge constructs, skills and dispositions within the subject disci-

Table 2.1 An option-less curriculum

S1–S3 and S4–S5 (i.e. the first five years of secondary education)
Pathway 1 (Core): Communication – L1 Language and Literature
Pathway 2 (Core): First Modern Foreign Language – L2 Language and Literature
Pathway 3 (Core): Second Modern Foreign Language – L3 Language and Literature
Pathway 4 (Core): Humanities
Pathway 5 (Core): Performance and Expressive Studies
Pathway 6 (Core): Science
Pathway 7 (Core): Social Studies
Pathway 8 (Core): Mathematics
S6–S7 (i.e. the last two years of secondary education)
Pathway 1 (Core): Communication – L1 Language and Literature; Integrated Themes: Reading, Writing, Speaking and Listening, Multi-modality, Knowledge about Language and Communication, ICT, and Language and Communication Dispositions
Pathway 2 (Core): First Modern Foreign Language – L2 Language and Literature; to include ONL Irish, Finnish, Maltese, Swedish; Integrated Themes: L2 Reading, L2 Writing, L2 Speaking and Listening, Knowledge about L2 Language and Communication, and L2 Language and Communication Dispositions
Pathway 3 (Core): Humanities; Integrated Themes: (These are not subjects but elements of subjects forming a Humanities Area of Study.) History, Geography, Religious Studies and Ethics, Ancient Civilizations, Fine Art and History of Art, Music History and Appreciation, Law, Archaeology, Architecture, and Philosophy
Pathway 4 (Core): Performance and Expressive Studies; Connected Themes: Music, Drama, Dance, Art and Design, and Physical Education
Pathway 5 (Core): Science; Integrated Themes: (These are not subjects but elements of subjects forming a Science Area of Study) Physics, Chemistry, Biology, Biochemistry, Biotechnology, Technology, including Computer Science, Earth Science, Astronomy, Medicine
Pathway 6 (Core): Social Studies; Integrated Themes: (These are not subjects but elements of subjects forming a Social Studies Area of Study.) Psychology, Sociology, Statistical Science, Economics, Business Studies, and Political Science
Pathway 7 (Core): Mathematics; Integrated Themes: Relations between quantities and algebraic expressions, Ratio and proportional reasoning, Connecting measurement and decimals, Spatial and geometrical reasoning, Reasoning about data, Reasoning about uncertainty, and Functional relations between variables
Pathway 8 (Core): Second Modern Foreign Language – L2 Language and Literature; to include ONL Irish, Finnish, Maltese, Swedish; Integrated Themes: L2 Reading, L2 Writing, L2 Speaking and Listening, Knowledge about L2 Language and Communication, and L2 Language and Communication Dispositions

pline) for each subject area. However, depending on the way subject content is chosen, arranged and taught within the pathway, this should not be thought of as necessarily resulting in a weakening of each subject area.

A second alternative is to retain the six curriculum pathways but instead of offering social studies, humanities or science as generic areas of study, each pathway is broken down into four, five or six subjects. Each student then chooses one option from each of the pathways. This is a curriculum with option choices within pathways (see Table 2.2). So, in the social studies pathway, students would choose between psychology, sociology, statistical science, economics, business studies and political science, with each of these subjects retaining its identity. If it was considered

Table 2.2 An option within pathways curriculum

S1–S3 and S4–S5 (i.e. the first five years of secondary education)
Pathway 1 Communication – L1 Language and Literature
Pathway 2 First Modern Foreign Language – L2 Language and Literature
Pathway 3 Second Modern Foreign Language – L3 Language and Literature
Pathway 4 Humanities
Pathway 5 Performance and Expressive Studies
Pathway 6 Science
Pathway 7 Social Studies
Pathway 8 Mathematics
S6–S7 (i.e. the last two years of secondary education)
Pathway 1 (Option 1): Mother Tongue Language L1 – Choice between Language, Literature and ICT
Pathway 2 (Option 2): First Modern Foreign Language – L2 Language and Literature – Choice between all the different European languages
Pathway 3 (Option 3): Humanities – Choice between History, Geography, Religious Studies and Ethics, Ancient Civilizations, Fine Art and History of Art, Music History and Appreciation, Law, Archaeology, Architecture, and Philosophy
Pathway 4 (Option 4): Performance and Expressive Studies – Choice between Music, Drama, Dance, Art and Design, and Physical Education
Pathway 5 (Option 5) Science – Choice between Physics, Chemistry, Biology, Biochemistry, Biotechnology, Technology, Computer Science, Earth Science, Astronomy, Medicine
Pathway 6 (Option 6) Social Studies – Choice between Psychology, Sociology, Statistical Science, Economics, Business Studies, and Political Science
Pathway 7 (Option 7) Mathematics – Choice between Elementary and Advanced Mathematics
Pathway 8 (Option 8) Second Modern Foreign Language – Choice between all the different European languages

that too small amounts of time or not enough lessons were being allocated to each subject, then the length of the school day could be increased to accommodate all the subjects being taught or time for one pathway could be increased at the expense of other pathways.

There are a number of advantages with this system. The eight competences are able genuinely to act as a guiding curriculum framework as they are mandated to. Students would be able to make better choices of which subjects they should study at university because they have studied one, or perhaps even two, subjects in each pathway. The curriculum of each individual student would have genuine breadth and be comprehensive in coverage. The problems associated with clashing options (i.e. having to choose between biology, ICT and geography when the student wants to study biology and ICT and has to settle for biology and history) and with option choices between subjects that are not compatible (i.e. choosing two options from biology, chemistry, ICT, physics and geography) would not exist. The principal disadvantage of this system is that coverage (i.e. exposure to the knowledge constructs, skills and dispositions) of the overall disciplinary pathway would be restricted (unless the amount of time given to the curriculum was increased). Further, this alternative and the first one would entail radical changes to the curriculum and there are extra costs and potential risks associated with it.

The third alternative is a mixture of core subjects and options (of different types and as having different relations with the core subjects), as in the current arrangements (see Tables 2.3 and 2.4). The organisation of secondary studies was the object of a broad reform in April 1990. Additional reforms to S1–S3, originally introduced as part of the current proposal for the reorganisation of secondary studies, were implemented in September 2014. The curricula for the three cycles in secondary school comprise, in differing proportions: core (compulsory) subjects, optional subjects and complementary subjects. For core subjects, non-viable group sizes are managed by grouping students across several levels (called 'vertical grouping') or across languages (called 'horizontal grouping'); if this is not possible teaching hours are reduced. A group is not considered viable if it has less than seven pupils for S1 to S5 and less than five for S6 and S7. Optional courses run in any given language only if there are a sufficient number of students selecting the option; for optional courses,

Table 2.3 Current arrangement of subjects S1–S5

S1–S3 (i.e. the first three years of secondary education) Subject 1 L1 (Years 1 and 2, five periods; Year 3, four periods) Subject 2 L2 (Year 1, five periods; Years 2 and 3, four periods) Subject 3 L3 (Year 1, five periods; Years 2 and 3, four periods) Subject 4 Human Sciences (Years 1, 2 and 3, four periods) Subject 5 Physical Education (Years 1, 2 and 3, four periods) Subject 6 Mathematics (Years 1, 2 and 4, four periods) Subject 7 Religion/Ethics (Years 1, 2 and 3, two periods) Subject 8 Integrated Science (Years 1, 2 and 3, four periods) Subject 9 Art (Years 1, 2 and 3, two periods) Subject 10 Music (Years 1, 2 and 3, two periods) Subject 11 ICT (Years 1 and 2, one period; Year 3, two periods – optional) Subject 12 Latin (Years 2 and 3 – optional) **S4–S5 (i.e. the next two years of secondary education)** Subject 1 L1 (Years 4 and 5, four periods) Subject 2 L2 (Years 4 and 5, three periods) Subject 3 L3 (Years 4 and 5, three periods) Subject 4 History (Years 4 and 5, two periods) Subject 5 Physical Education (Years 4 and 5, two periods) Subject 6 Mathematics (Years 4 and 5, either four or six periods) Subject 7 Religion/Ethics (Years 4 and 5, one period) Subject 8 Geography (Years 4 and 5, two periods) Subject 9 Physics (Years 4 and 5, two periods) Subject 10 Biology (Years 4 and 5, two periods) Subject 11 Chemistry (Years 4 and 5, two periods) Subject 12 Art (Years 4 and 5, two periods – optional) Subject 13 Music (Years 4 and 5, two periods – optional) Subject 14 ICT (Years 4 and 5, two periods – optional) Subject 15 Latin (Years 4 and 5, two periods – optional) Subject 16 Greek/Ancient Greek (Years 4 and 5, four/two periods – optional) Subject 17 L4 (Years 4 and 5, four periods – optional) Subject 18 Economics (Years 4 and 5, four periods – optional)

students are often given the choice to take the course in a vehicular language, if it is offered.

Currently, the number of courses using a student's 'non-dominant' language (i.e. not L1) as the language of instruction increases as the student progresses into secondary school. In particular, by the end of the first cycle of secondary school and into the second cycle there is a marked increase in the number of courses taught in L2; in the second cycle, options are also added, which likewise increases the chance of students

Table 2.4 S6–S7 Current arrangement of studies (i.e. last two years of secondary education)

Core subjects		Options		Complementary subject
Column 1 (periods)	Column 2[a] (periods)	Column 3 (periods)	Column 4[b] (periods)	Column 5[c] (periods)
L1 (4 periods)	Biology (2 periods)	Latin (4 periods)	Advanced L1 (3 periods)	Lab-Physics (2 periods)
L2 (3 periods)	History (2 periods)	Greek (4 periods)	Advanced L2 (3 periods)	Lab-Chem (2 periods)
Mathematics (3/5 periods)	Geography (2 periods)	Philosophy (4 periods)	Advanced Maths (3 periods)	Lab-Bio (2 periods)
Religion/Ethics (1 period)	Philosophy (2 periods)	L3 (4 periods)		Computing (2 periods)
Physical Education (2 periods)		L4 (4 periods)		Elementary Economics (2 periods)
		History (4 periods)		Sociology (2 periods)
		Geography (4 periods)		Art (2 periods)
		Economics (4 periods)		Music (2 periods)
		Physics (4 periods)		Sport (2 periods)
		Chemistry (4 periods)		
		Biology (4 periods)		
		Art (4 periods)		
		Music (4 periods)		

[a] These courses must be taken if not chosen in column 3. Biology is compulsory unless Physics, Chemistry or Biology is chosen in column 3
[b] Advanced Maths only with 5-period Maths in column 1
[c] Art, Music and Economics not allowed if taken in column 3

(particularly in smaller language sections) taking courses in their L2 or other vehicular language. Progression is meant to follow students' linguistic development, i.e. by S3 students are believed to be equipped with the skills to learn academic subjects in their L2.

In the current structure, students have some degree of personal choice over how much of their secondary education they undertake in their L2 or other languages. However, in most instances they are only able to exercise this control by confining their choice of subject options according to the specified language of instruction. This situation may favour multilingual students, but it can create difficulties for students who are not linguistically able due to learning difficulties or late entry into the system, and this is quite common given the mobility of the target population between countries and systems of education. There is also a wide range of experiences depending on the size or viability of the language section to which the student belongs, with students in smaller sections more often compelled to take courses in vehicular languages.

The proposals developed for the reorganisation of the upper secondary cycle (S6–S7) in February 2012 (cf. Board of Governors 2012) were the most far reaching and have thus been the most divisive. These were also the most thoroughly analysed by the working group, parents and other stakeholders. The current structure at S6–S7 is organised along the following lines (see Table 2.4). Core subjects must be offered. Options and complementary subjects may be offered if there are enough students in a section or school interested. (The minimum number of students required to create a course at this level is five). Some subjects are offered at both basic (2 periods, 3 for mathematics) and advanced levels (4 periods, 5 for mathematics). These include: mathematics, biology, history, geography and philosophy. Physics and chemistry are offered only in 4 period blocks (no 2-period option is offered). It is compulsory to choose history, geography and philosophy, either at a basic or at a superior level. It is compulsory to choose at least one scientific subject, i.e. biology, physics or chemistry. The possible choices are restricted by the Baccalaureate written and oral examination rules.

Any route through this complicated arrangement means that some form of specialisation prior to S6 and S7 is inevitable. Students are confronted with choices between disparate sets of options and even then, depending on the size of the school, the number of students opting for particular subjects, the types of L1 students choosing these subjects and the possibility of forming groupings within each school to accommodate this, they may not be given their first choices and thus have to settle for subjects which they did not choose.

With these arrangements, the following problems remain with regards to students' curricular arrangements: early specialisation; choosing between subjects which are not related; choosing between subjects which are related with the consequence that students are likely to be disappointed if they want to specialise in the humanities, the natural sciences or the social sciences; because of the arrangement of resources within the system or within the school (i.e. size of classes, L1 distributions of students, possibility of vertical groupings) they may be denied their first choices, with consequent effects on their motivation and the quality of their work; and by designating some subject areas as 2 period (restricted curriculum) or 4 period (extended curriculum) or 4 period plus (supplementary curriculum), different levels of learning and different types of students are created. This complicates and may distort the process of progression through a subject-based curriculum.

Traditionally courses at S6 to S7 level have been offered as core and elective modules. There are a number of reasons for this. In order to accommodate a broad and comprehensive curriculum conceived in strongly classified terms (i.e. where there are clear boundaries between subject areas), the only possible arrangements that can be made are to cluster some subjects together and offer choices within those clusters. This has the disadvantage that the clusters and the core subject areas, unless they are carefully designed, may not offer a comprehensive coverage of the curriculum and may allow a neglect of some of the key elements of the curriculum. For example, unless the core (which might include compulsory and clusters of optional subjects) is understood as having an overarching rationale, then it may not be fully comprehensive. What this means is that some students, especially those who specialise early, will be taught with a narrower curriculum.

There is always a problem with moving from traditional curriculum arrangements to new ones, because teachers, parents and students have over a period of time developed a familiarity with these arrangements, and change is always unsettling. There is also the issue that changing the arrangements for the curriculum may act to reduce the credibility of the European Baccalaureate and thus put at risk students' ability to access higher education. Another implication of changing the curriculum arrangements from a system that allows some choice, to one in which there is little choice, is that this reduced specialisation limits students' capacity to make choices for themselves and to study subjects and areas of the curriculum which have a special interest for them. This could have a negative effect on the motivation of the students.

Curriculum Reforms

A curriculum in essence is a planned programme of learning, and therefore if we are to understand it, we also have to develop a theory of learning. As a concept, learning is fundamentally related to knowledge, and therefore if we are thinking about learning and the practices of learning, we also need to make reference to what is to be and how it is learned, and typically what we are aiming at in such considerations is some form of knowledge. Philosophers usually divide knowledge into two principal categories, knowing-that and knowing-how. (They sometimes also add a third category, knowing-by-acquaintance, but this is not central to the argument that is being made.) The suggestion here is that these forms of knowledge are fundamentally different; in other words, there are strong and impermeable boundaries between them. Using a formulation from Robert Brandom (2000), we want to suggest that this is misleading, and that consequently some of the problems that these strong insulations have created can be resolved. This has implications for our theory of learning and knowledge-development and therefore for our curriculum theory that follows from it. What also follows from this is that in society these different forms of knowledge are given different statuses or have different attachments of importance, so, for example, vocational knowledge (broadly thought of as being about processes) is considered to be less important than academic knowledge (broadly understood as being about propositions), but these ascriptions of importance do not lie in the intrinsic nature of each knowledge form but in the way these knowledge forms are realised in particular societies.

Knowledge then, is fundamental to the three types of learning that have been identified: cognitive (relating to propositions), skill-based (relating to processes) and dispositional (relating to embodiments). Cognition comprises the manipulation of those symbolic resources (words, numbers, pictures etc.), which points to (though not necessarily in a mirroring or isomorphic sense) something outside itself, though the referent might also be construed as internally-related, or more specifically, as a part of an already established network of concepts (for example, cf. Brandom 2000). Skill-based knowledge is different from cognition because it is procedural and not propositional. Dispositional knowledge refers to relatively stable habits of mind and body, sensitivities to occasion and participation repertoires. Distinguishing between knowledge of how to do something (or process forms of knowledge), knowledge of something (or, in Brandom's terms, judging that claim in terms of its relations within and to a network of concepts) and embodied forms of knowledge (assimilating an action and being able to perform in the spaces associated with that action) is important; however, they are in essence all knowledge-making activities, and furthermore as we will see can be formulated generically as acts of learning.

Knowledge is transformed at the pedagogic site, so it is possible to suggest that qualities such as: the simulation of the learning object, the representational mode of the object, its degree and type of amplification, control in the pedagogic relationship, progression or its relations with other learning objects (i.e. curriculum integration), the type of pedagogic text, relations with other people in the learning process, the organization of time (temporal relations) and types of feedback mechanism are fundamental components of this pedagogic transformation. What this means is that in the learning process, the learning object takes a new form as a result of changes to its properties: simulation, representation, amplification, control, integration, textual form, relations with other people, time and feedback. In contrast to some frameworks, i.e. Bernstein's sociolinguistic code theory (2002) or Maton's (2014) knowledge and knowers thesis, the sheer complexity of the possible pedagogic knowledge forms that this allows means that relations between pedagogic arrangements and social arrangements, and between these pedagogic arrangements and notions of identity-formation and social positioning, can only be tentatively sketched out.

Theoretical and contextual considerations impact, then, on how elements of teaching and learning are realised. Acknowledging this allows the identification of a number of learning models: assessment for learning, observation, coaching, goal-clarification, mentoring, peer learning, simulation, instruction, concept-formation, reflection, meta-cognitive learning, problem solving, and practice. And each of these in turn is underpinned by a particular theory of learning. What this means is that any model of learning that is employed is constructed in relation to particular views of how we can know the world and what it is. These models or learning sets (and this includes feedback mechanisms of a particular kind) give different emphases to the various elements of a learning process.

Choosing between these models depends on the nature and constitution of the learning object; in other words, the former is logically dependent on the latter. It also depends on the choice of learning theory that is made. These learning models have a crucial role to play (whichever one is chosen) in processes of learning and constitute elements of Bernstein's (2000) pedagogic device. In Chap. 3 we examine the organisation of language learning and the development of intercultural competence in the European school system.

Open Access This chapter is licensed under the terms of the Creative Commons Attribution 4.0 International License (http://creativecommons.org/licenses/by/4.0/), which permits use, sharing, adaptation, distribution and reproduction in any medium or format, as long as you give appropriate credit to the original author(s) and the source, provide a link to the Creative Commons license and indicate if changes were made.

The images or other third party material in this chapter are included in the chapter's Creative Commons license, unless indicated otherwise in a credit line to the material. If material is not included in the chapter's Creative Commons license and your intended use is not permitted by statutory regulation or exceeds the permitted use, you will need to obtain permission directly from the copyright holder.

3

Educated Side by Side: The Role of Language in the European Schools

Language learning and intercultural communication are at the core of the European schools' genesis and ethos. The schools are a success story in that the European schools' network continues to grow. Graduates are not only proficient in their L1, but have achieved a sufficient degree of fluency in an L2 to have successfully studied content subjects such as history through their L2 and sometimes their L3. All European schools' students study an L3. Students work and learn with and from teachers and other students who come from diverse nationalities. Longstanding structural arrangements such as the organisation of the teaching of a minimum of three languages including the L1, the right to establish L1 language sections where numbers warrant it, the requirement to study some subjects through an L2, and the mixing of students from diverse nationalities have all helped school graduates to work side by side and become multilingual. The chapter recognises this success, but will above all explore ways to bring greater clarity and substance to the European schools' current organisation of learning to enhance language learning and the development of intercultural competence. The previously discussed premise of a curriculum, which includes an intelligible set of specifications expressed as learning standards or objects, as the principal driver of educational reform will serve as a key lens for the discussion.

© The Author(s) 2018
S. Leaton Gray et al., *Curriculum Reform in the European Schools*,
https://doi.org/10.1007/978-3-319-71464-6_3

Language Policy

Language policy elements are to be found in numerous European schools' policy prescriptions (e.g. mission statement, General Rules of the European Schools, Provision of Educational Support in the European Schools – procedural document, Reform of the European Schools System, Proposal of the 'Organisation of Studies in the Secondary Cycle' Working Group, Control of the Level of Linguistic Competence as Part of the Procedure for Recruitment of Non-native Speaker Teaching and Educational Support Staff, Languages of Tuition for Economics in the European Schools System, and language and content subject syllabuses). Policy is also being developed *in situ* through the interpretation of existing policies (e.g. discussions of whether and in which school in Brussels an Estonian language section will be opened). The policy is embodied in and realised through a series of mechanisms or structural arrangements: language sections that support learning through the L1 in cases where the number of students is sufficient; special provisions for SWALS; the obligatory delivery of some content subjects through the students' L2 (and possibly L3); and language courses in L1, L2, L3, L4 and L5.

Despite the fact that language learning and intercultural communication are at the core of the European schools' ethos, there is no one place the European schools' internal and external stakeholders can turn to for understanding the nature of multilingual education in the European Schools, for an overview of the aims of language learning, or for direction on how language policy translates into teaching and learning practices. Existing policy documents including curriculum documents provide scant direction on how teaching and learning practices at the European schools are expected to promote high degrees of language learning, or content and language learning whilst learning through a first, second and third language.

Typically bilingual education supports individuals in becoming and remaining bilingual. At least two languages are used to teach different content subjects such as mathematics or history for several years. Languages are also taught in language classes. If students are to be well placed in continuing to develop their second and first language proficiency after graduation both languages would be used as media of instruction throughout the final years of school life. Bilingual education aims to support students in developing age and grade-appropriate levels of:

- L1 competence in reading, writing, speaking, and listening;
- advanced functional proficiency in L2 reading, writing, speaking and listening;
- academic achievement in all school content subjects, such as Mathematics and Science taught primarily through the L2 and in those taught primarily through the L1;
- levels of understanding and appreciation of the culture of the L1 group, and of the L2 group(s); and, promotes
- capacity for and interest in inter-cultural communication (Mehisto 2012).

A bilingual education programme can support students in learning additional languages; however, it would not be referred to as a trilingual or multilingual education programme if students were not afforded an opportunity to learn content subjects through three or more languages. Thus, the European schools can be considered above all a bilingual education system that seeks to foster multilingual proficiency among its graduates.

In general, languages are considered interdependent. Students are likely to transfer L1 skills and knowledge to their L2 and L3 and vice versa. The greater a student's L1 proficiency, the greater his or her metalinguistic awareness, and the better his or her L1 language learning habits and skills, the more likely it is that this proficiency, metalinguistic awareness and these language learning habits and skills will support the learning of the L2 and the L3 and through the L2 and L3 (cf. Cummins 1997, 2013). Moreover, 'cognition and language create each other' (Ellis and Robinson 2008). This means that deeper order thinking and meaning making are also dependent 'on the development of advanced literacy skills' (Cammarata et al. 2016). Hence bilingual education is expected to focus on the development of high degrees of literacy skills in both the L1 and the L2. In order to support the development of high degrees of bi-literacy successful bilingual education programmes foster cooperation between teachers teaching through the students' L1 and L2 (Genesee and Hamayan 2016).

The lack of a European Schools' overarching language policy document is problematic at both the systemic and classroom levels. It implies that bilingual and multicultural education are not being led in a systematic manner with clearly stated goals. A key characteristic of successful bilingual education systems is having a well-defined purpose, goals, standards and plans pertaining to both content and language learning and this in all classes. Cloud et al. (2000: 10) argue that these must all be '(a) understood, (b) accepted, and (c) implemented in a coherent fashion by all educational and support personnel in the programme'. This aligns with Fullan's (2001) previously discussed view that it is essential to have high degrees of coherence across vision statements, plans and polices, and this in particular during an education reform effort. Moreover, the lack of a language policy document suggests that there is no concerted effort to help all educators (no matter the language of instruction) to understand the specificities of working in a bilingual education context. Commonly held knowledge by school staff of these specificities is considered a hallmark of successful bilingual education systems (Fortune and Tedick 2014). Teachers need to understand how pedagogy changes in bilingual education contexts. For example, all teachers are expected to support content and language learning, but content teachers on several continents have difficulty assuming the dual role of teaching both content and language (Gajo 2007; Genesee 2008), while language teachers often find it difficult to use a content-based approach (Martel 2016). In other words, the pedagogical principles are not self-evident, and in particular secondary school teachers tend not to be prepared to apply best practices in bilingual education without first receiving considerable training and support. In addition, the theoretical equality of esteem accorded to all official EU languages at the European schools is in practice not fully achieved. Some languages, such as the three official ones, English, French and German, enjoy greater status than others. Not all parents fully appreciate the value of educating their children through their L1.

In order to help address some of the above concerns, a language policy, we suggest, could include some or all of the following elements: an introduction or preamble; aims; connections to European School values and other policies; a description of the role of language learning (including for L1, L2, L3, L4 and L5); in-class and out-of-class language use in classes taught through the L1 and L2; in-class and out-of-class language use in mixed language groups; core pedagogical principles; core intercultural competences; management implications; student support services; staff support services; staff professional development; student assessment; measures for raising awareness of language issues; an explanation of how and when the policy will be reviewed; and a glossary of key terms (e.g. bilingualism, trilingualism, multilingualism, plurilingualism, multilingual teaching, multicultural education, intercultural competence).

More specifically, for example, in relation to pedagogical principles, the policy would provide details of core practices that all teachers would be expected to apply. These might include the requirement to integrate content and language instruction in all classes through the concurrent articulation of clear, explicit and visible intended content and language learning objectives/outcomes, and the regular analysis of progress made in achieving these objectives. This analysis would involve the use of assessment as a tool for learning content and language, and for supporting students in developing related learning skills. The ultimate purpose of helping students to become assessment literate in reference to content and language learning is to contribute to their development as engaged and autonomous learners of both. The co-construction of learning environments by teachers and students that are safe, supportive and engaging, and that encourage rich verbal and written student output would also be a common practice in bilingual education as students need support in managing the added stress and cognitive load of learning through additional languages. The concurrent scaffolding of both content and language learning, and critical thinking is one means for achieving this. Finally, the use of differentiation, including for enrichment, for students at various stages on their content and language learning pathways would be a vital policy element particularly in the European schools with their diverse and somewhat transient student populations.

With regards to managing language practices, the proposed language policy, we suggest, could articulate guiding principles such as: expectations regarding content learning and bilingualism, trilingualism and/or multilingualism as they relate to school principals, teachers, and students; a commitment to build actively the status of all school languages; the expectation that all teachers are teachers of both content and language, and that management practices (e.g. professional development, performance reviews, inspections) support teachers in assuming this dual role; a commitment to ensure that the language needs of each student will be assessed in order to develop, as required, individual learning pathways; and that assessment for learning will be used to support content and language learning in all classes including those taught through the L1. Finally, this part of the policy could describe mechanisms that will be used to encourage language and content teachers to co-operate, and for teachers to co-operate across languages.

How any such policy is developed and approved will also be central to whether it will be well understood, accepted and implemented. Following on from the discussion in Chap. 1, if this change is to have the desired impact, the policy would need to be developed through a stakeholder inclusive process with external advice from language education experts. The policy would need to be widely discussed and communicated so key stakeholders were aware of, understood and supported it. The policy would need to become part of the work culture meaning that it is discussed in planning meetings and progress in implementation is systematically evaluated and reported on. Policy-related short and long-term wins would need to be identified and celebrated. Finally over time, the policy should be revised and enhanced to ensure it is fit for purpose and that stakeholders remain committed to its implementation.

Intercultural Competence

It is the mission of the European Schools to provide 'a multilingual and multicultural education for nursery, primary and secondary level students' that should, according to Jean Monnet's 1953 vision, help 'bring into being a united and thriving Europe'. Monnet's vision implies a high expectation where Europeans work side by side across languages and cultures to build a united and thriving Europe; however, the terms *multilingual* and *multicultural* are not defined by the European Schools. The definition of these and other related terms reveal that developing proficiency in a language is inextricably tied to the development of intercultural competence.

The Commission of the European Communities (European Commission 2007: 6) defines multilingualism as 'the ability of societies, institutions, groups and individuals to engage, on a regular basis, with more than one language in their day-to-day lives'. The European Commission (2005: 3) also refers to multilingualism as 'the co-existence of different language communities in one geographical area'. Thus, for the European Commission (EC) multilingualism focuses on the co-existence of and the regular engagement with more than one language in one territory. Language is not problematised, but rather it is presented as a positive, or, at the very least, neutral force in the co-existence of people at an individual, group, institutional and societal level. This broad definition embraces both the concepts of multilingualism and plurilingualism as defined by the Council of Europe, which makes a distinction between multilingualism as a description of social organisation, and plurilingualism as an individual linguistic and cultural competence in more than one language and culture. The Council of Europe defines plurilingualism as the ability:

> to use languages for the purposes of communication and to take part in intercultural action, where a person, viewed as a social agent, has proficiency, of varying degrees, in several languages and experience of several cultures. This ability is concretised in a repertoire of languages a speaker can use. (Council of Europe 2007a: 17)

This definition stresses the ability and the responsibility of the plurilingual individual to bridge the multilingual social order. A plurilingual individual is not only defined in linguistic terms, but is considered capable of crossing both a linguistic and cultural divide, having linguistic and cultural competences that are evidenced by intercultural communication and enrichment. Plurilingual co-existence includes a process of cross-fertilisation or 'intercultural action' (ibid.).

> The language learner becomes plurilingual and develops interculturality. The linguistic and cultural competences in respect of each language are modified by knowledge of the other and contribute to inter-cultural awareness, skills and know-how. They enable the individual to develop an enriched, more complex personality and an enhanced capacity for further language learning and greater openness to new cultural experiences. (Council of Europe 2007b: 43)

This definition includes social and intercultural competences that are an essential element of communication through different languages. The same can be assumed for the European Commission's definition of multilingualism. Language and intercultural skills are central to the European project. The European Union has established a goal of 'mother tongue plus two other languages for all' its citizens (European Commission 2003: 7). Moreover, the European Commission (2017) has recently reiterated the need to develop a new narrative that stresses that 'the EU is not solely about the economy and growth, but also about cultural unity and common values in a globalised world.' This signals a possible shift away from euro-centric intercultural competence to a more global view of multilingual and intercultural competence. This aligns with the findings of Eccles and Gootman (2002), who argue that, in an era of globalisation, in-depth knowledge of more than one culture is considered a vital part of the cognitive development of young people.

The fact that the European Schools have not defined key terms such as multilingualism or culture, or drawn out what constitutes intercultural competence, does not appear to have deterred support for the schools. Parents have praised 'the multicultural and European citizen spirit brought by the multilingual education of European Schools' as one of its most appreciated features (Leaton Gray et al. 2015: 10). The number of schools in the network continues to grow. It is generally assumed that multilingual education is the vehicle 'of intercultural education' and 'that acquiring a deep knowledge and an active command of languages other than one's mother tongue has the effect of expanding the mind and enhancing intercultural competence' (Allemann-Ghionda 2012: 126). The assumption implies that intercultural competence may be an incidental side effect of multilingual education. A review of a cross-section of the European Schools curriculum documents confirms that culture and intercultural competences have not been defined in detail in any given subject curriculum or in a school wide policy document (Leaton Gray et al. 2015). However, the fact that history and geography are taught as of the third year of secondary school in the students' L2 by teachers who most likely do not share their nationality does at least create an opportunity to foster a broadening of the students' ability to view issues from different perspectives (an intercultural competence). Still, the decisions on what constitutes intercultural competence, and whether, and if so how, it should be explicitly taught appear to be left to individual teachers.

We suggest that by centrally defining terms such as *culture* or at the very least including an exploration of several definitions of the term *culture*, the European schools would be better placed to support students and teachers in developing a substantially richer understanding of the term, which in turn could contribute to a more nuanced understanding of intercultural competence. UNESCO (2001) defines culture in its Universal Declaration on Cultural Diversity as follows:

> Culture is the set of distinctive spiritual, material, intellectual and emotional features of society or a social group, and that it encompasses, in addition to art and literature, lifestyles, ways of living together, value systems, traditions and beliefs. (UNESCO 2001)

The above definition along with a review of other well-known definitions could serve as a reference point in exploring elements of culture. For example, in order to help students to engage with culture as a concept and to deepen their cultural knowledge all subject curricula could draw to a lesser or greater extent on some of the following often interrelated categories – abandoned practices, architecture, art (fine and applied), attitudes, beliefs, concepts of the universe, cuisine, custom, education, emigration, environmental protection, events, experience, famous people, film, friendship, games, hierarchies, history, humour, immigration, informal governing arrangements, insults, knowledge, legislation, literature, material objects/artefacts, media, music, notions of time, personal space, politics, politeness, possessions, practices, prejudice, proverbs, public institutions, queuing, religion, rituals, role of nature, roles, soap operas, social security, social class, spatial relations, sports, stereotypes, taboos, trends, values, ways of giving and receiving feedback, and work. This would be, in particular, the case with, but not limited to, language curricula. It is noteworthy that culture resides not in the above elements per se, but in how individuals and groups interpret, use and perceive these constructs (Banks and McGee 1989). We caution that many of the above are complex constructs, and need to be approached with care, with knowledge-building and perspective-taking being key parts of the exploration process. A discussion of personal values can help centre discussions. Moreover, it can be helpful to often return to the fact that no cultural construct is likely to be a monolithic symbol embraced by all members of a language community, and that culture is dynamic and therefore constantly changing and hopefully progressing.

More importantly, we argue that if an education system has set itself the mission of offering a multicultural education, and if it wishes to help students develop intercultural competence it needs to move beyond the assumption that this will occur simply through the provision of multilingual education. 'Language fluency is necessary but in itself insufficient to represent intercultural competence' (Deardorff 2014: 1). A definition of core intercultural competences and related learning intentions is also required. These could provide teachers with a focus for course development. They could also support students in reflecting on and building intercultural competence by helping to set and measure progress in achieving related targets. Furthermore, declared curricular intentions related to intercultural competence could help convey instructional intent to parents and other stakeholders, and provide a reference point for course evaluations and improvements.

A major challenge in such a process is that these competences are often not immediately apparent (Meyer 2014). Hence, we make explicit below some intercultural competences in order to highlight the complexities involved in developing intercultural competence and to stress that a more systematic approach is required. At its core, intercultural competence is about perspective-taking. Broadly speaking it consists of 'the appropriate and effective management of interaction between people who, to some degree or another, represent different or divergent affective, cognitive and behavioral orientations to the world' (Spitzberg and Changnon 2009: 9). When intercultural competences are broken down into more tangible elements, they are usually divided into three or four interrelated categories: knowledge, skills, attitudes and values. Values are sometimes subsumed under knowledge and attitudes.

In the knowledge domain, Candelier et al. (2012) propose that students need to know that it is often difficult to distinguish one culture from another, and that a culture is always complex and is itself made up of (more or less) different and conflicting or convergent subcultures. This leads to the idea that one can have a multiple, plural or composite identity. In other words, every person forms part of at least one cultural community and many persons form part of more than one cultural community. This seems particularly pertinent in the European schools' context. On a practical level, students need knowledge of some of the characteristics of their own situation and cultural environment. They also need to know some social practices and customs from different cultures, including some norms related to social practices, which are specific to certain social, regional and generational groupings. Cultural practices vary across and within generational, regional and social groupings. Students also need to know how culture and identity influence communicative interactions. Finally, they need to know strategies that one can use to resolve intercultural conflicts, such as knowing that the causes of misunderstanding must be sought out and clarified in common. In addition, Gudykunst (1993) proposes that students also need knowledge of alternative interpretations so they can weigh them against each other. They also require knowledge of 'oppressions' including 'intersecting oppressions' (e.g. class, gender, race, religion) (Spitzberg and Changnon 2009: 11).

In the attitudinal domain intercultural competences include: viewing difference as a learning opportunity; being prepared to be considered as an 'outsider'; being open (and mastering one's own eventual resistances) to what seems incomprehensible and different; having the will to suspend one's judgment, acquired representations and/or prejudices; considering all languages as equal in dignity; being disposed to plurilingual and pluricultural socialisation; seeing loans from cultures as contributing to cultural enrichment; being prepared to experience a threat to one's identity; being able to assume a critical distance from information and opinions produced by media, common sense and one's interlocutors about one's own community and other communities; being willing to construct 'informed' knowledge or representations; being willing to establish a relationship of equality in plurilingual and pluricultural interaction; and being open and empathetic towards the unfamiliar, be that linguistic or cultural (Candelier et al. 2012).

The skills domain includes the ability: to recognise and identify cultural specificities, references or affiliations; to view and interpret the world from other cultures' points of view and to analyse the cultural origin of different aspects of communication; to analyse the cultural origins of certain behaviours, and analyse misunderstandings due to cultural differences; to tolerate ambiguity and view it as a positive experience; to use formulae of politeness appropriately in diverse cultural contexts; to identify, analyse and reduce ethnocentrism; to compare one's own non-verbal communication practices with those of others and to explore one's own prejudices; to recognise and name cultural prejudice; to build well informed and structured arguments about cultural diversity; and to have conflict resolutions skills (ibid.). In addition, Spitzberg and Changnon (2009) argue that intercultural competence requires skill in identifying and challenging discriminatory acts, as well as skill in assessing intercultural performance.

In the values domain, intercultural competence includes valuing human dignity and human rights, cultural diversity, democracy, justice, fairness, equality and the rule of law (Council of Europe 2016). Deardorff (2013) adds to this list by suggesting that global intercultural competence includes: adaptation, cultural humility, listening, relationship building, respect, seeing from multiple perspectives, and self-awareness. Stressing the challenges of applying some of these competences, Spitzberg and Changnon (2009: 35) point out that as one seeks to adapt to diverse cultural situations, this should not 'result in excessive compromise of personal identity'. As people often draw their energy for action from the values and attitudinal domains it is these domains that fuel the implementation of knowledge through the use of mechanisms and the application of skills (Mehisto 2015).

This detailing of intercultural competences has sought to bring weight to the argument that the European Schools System could benefit from making explicit the intercultural competences it is seeking to develop. We suggest that the construct of intercultural competence is so complex it is not likely to be well understood across the European schools if curriculum documents do not make reference to it and draw it out in greater detail through related intended learning outcomes. Furthermore, without distilling these competences in one document and/or integrating some of these competences into curricula it is difficult to understand how leadership in the development of these competences could be assumed. It is difficult to support people in reaching a target if the target is unclear.

Language Curricula

The English, French and German L2 European schools' secondary level language syllabuses, with the exception of the very short L2 French and English syllabuses, appear light on content and heavy on language learning (Leaton Gray et al. 2015). This runs counter to current professional discourse on effective language teaching. Martel (2016: 107) argues that a language class should not be 'a thinking-light subject' focussed primarily on the learning of grammatical structures, and that language teachers choose content and tasks that are 'thought-provoking'. When content and tasks in language classes 'are not just an excuse to increase a learner's overall linguistic repertoire', but are also focussed on the 'acquisition of new knowledge as well as the completion of specifically targeted tasks designed to deepen students' understanding', capacity to think critically and learning of 'non-linguistic content', students and even teachers have much to gain (Cammarata 2016: 124).

Language classes that incorporate new meaningful content expose students to a wider range of topics and contexts than would be the case in a standard language class. Content-based language teaching uses more functions, genres, and registers of language and vocabulary (including terminology, phraseology and other formulaic sequences, collocations, connectives, phrasal verbs). By extension this will help students build their capacity to produce a deeper and wider range of language output (Cumming and Lyster 2016). Importantly in the European schools' context, where students need to use their L2 and in some cases their L3 as a medium for content learning, content-rich language classes would likely provide them with exposure to and practice in using the general academic language that is needed in several content subjects. However, a review of the European schools' secondary level English, French and German L2 language syllabuses reveal that these language classes could do more to help prepare students for those content subjects they are expected to study through their L2 (Leaton Gray et al. 2015). More specifically, they could further incorporate meaningful activities that require the use of core academic functions common to many content subjects such as: analysing, classifying, comparing, contrasting, explaining causes and consequences, evaluating, hypothesising, inquiring collaboratively, justifying, persuading, separating fact from opinion, solving problems, synthesising and verifying.

A further benefit of content-based language instruction as opposed to standard language teaching is that curricular content becomes more meaningful and this creates 'a genuine immediate need to learn the language', which in turn engages and motivates students to learn language (Lightbown and Spada 2013: 193). The more meaningful the content the more likely students are to recall the related language. Increased recall can boost student confidence in using the language. As a by-product, anxiety related to language use and learning is usually reduced. As an added benefit to content-based instruction in language classes, teachers report finding their own work more motivating (Davison and Williams 2001). Importantly when language classes focus on integrating meaningful content and encouraging students to think critically about that content, the students become more effective critical thinkers in reference to both content and language. This implies avoiding situations where language teachers focus only on the language being learned and avoid substantive analysis of the content used to carry the language (Cammarata et al. 2016).

European schools' secondary level students have an immediate need to use their L2 (in some cases their L3) to navigate, to think critically about and to learn content in geography, history, and economics classes. This reality places an extra responsibility for language learning on the L2 and L3 language teachers. It is reasonable to expect language curricula and teaching to adapt to this reality. This would mean adapting L2 and L3 language curricula so as to teach elements of language in a sequence that is partly determined by the content students are learning through their L2 and/or L3. L1 language teachers would also be expected to play a supportive role in helping students develop generic language skills and high levels of literacy. Furthermore, as there is a general consensus that content-based language learning leads to greater language learning, it is also reasonable to expect that language classes engage students with new and meaningful content in addition to new language (Brinton et al. 2011; Tedick and Wesely 2015).

There are several ways of incorporating meaningful content into language classes. As we discussed in the previous section on intercultural competence, in particular considering the centrality of culture and intercultural competence in the European schools' discourse, it would be logical to integrate more substantive cultural content and the development of intercultural competences into language curricula. This would be the case even with curricula such as the Finnish L4 syllabus, which has sought to unpack Finnish culture in relative detail. In addition, language curricula could use topics and materials that are compatible with what is being learned in content classes. This content-compatible material would not be essential for students to meet the intended content learning outcomes of their content classes, but help students develop a command of the language needed to meet those content outcomes. Language teachers would need to feel comfortable in using and teaching these content compatible topics and materials. These are generally integrated into language classes through cooperation between content and language teachers. Another option is to encourage enquiry-based learning where students research a topic both in their L1 and L2 and report on it in their L2. Enquiry learning places part of the onus on the student to seek out and use needed language, whilst peers and teachers would then be called on to provide corrective feedback.

Reagan (2016) suggests that language teachers should use critical pedagogies in language classes; a pedagogy focussed on reducing inequalities and injustices. He proposes that they explore with students 'fundamental questions about knowledge, justice, equity in their own classroom, school, family and community'. Reagan (2016: 174 citing Wink 2000) contends that by having students engage with 'understanding their place and responsibility within' the world in order to improve it, they become truly engaged with thinking critically about content and language that reaches beyond the walls of the classroom. He sees critical pedagogy as a way of making content and language learning 'count' and thus memorable.

A major exercise in coherence making would need to take place if the above-suggested changes were to be incorporated in the European schools' language curricula. Curriculum documents would need to be revised through a stakeholder inclusive process. The development of L2 and L3 language curricula would to some extent need to be aligned with the curricula of those subjects students are studying through their L2 and /or L3. A discussion would be required on the teaching practices that support learning in bilingual education contexts. For example, in situations where students are not fluent speakers of a given medium of instruction, Gibbons (2009) argues that when planning for a curriculum of intellectual quality, there is a need to maintain a relentless double focus on building a high-challenge, high-support learning environment. Also, assessment procedures would need to be adjusted to make sure they support the achievement of curricular goals. Finally, as moving to a content-based approach in language classrooms is likely to constitute a major shift in practice, it is best to assume that this change will not be self-evident to students, their parents, language teachers, content teachers or school administrators. Key stakeholders would need to have their attention drawn to the fact that language classes now support not only language learning, but content learning and critical thinking and that students need to maintain a triple focus in language classes on language, content and precision of thought. This would require additional effort from, and the use of effective learning strategies by, students. Teachers would likely require professional development. Finally, this proposed shift also calls for cooperation with content teachers and a 'language-sensitive' approach to teaching in content classes (Wolff 2011).

Content Subject Curricula

The primary intent of teaching some subjects in the European schools through the students' L2 is that students become more proficient in that L2. In other words, in addition to teaching students content, those subjects taught through the students' L2 are being used as a vehicle for language teaching and learning. However, the generally longstanding European schools' subject syllabuses do not include explicit language objectives. Neither do new syllabuses such as the Geography Syllabus (4 period course Year 6/7) and ICTC Syllabus (S1–S3 ICT). This leaves the impression that language learning in content classes is seen as largely incidental. Language that needs to be learned is rarely drawn out in curriculum documents, and when this is done, it is at the level of vocabulary (e.g. new Geography syllabus). Subject specific terminology can be considered only the tip of the iceberg in terms of the academic language of Geography that must be learned by students. The syllabuses for content subjects to be taught through the L1 also lack well-defined language objectives.

Language plays a crucial role in learning. '[L]anguage, communication and cognition […] are mutually inextricable. Cognition and language create each other' (Ellis and Robinson 2008: 3). From a Vygotskian perspective, language is not simply a tool for communication, it is a tool for creating knowledge through 'socially shared cognition' (Kasper 2008: 59), and for honing thinking (Vygotsky 1978). Thus, thinking does not simply occur in a vacuum, but requires input from and interaction with others. If language assumes a double function, 'as a means for communication and a tool for thinking', it is also possible to view both interactions in the L1 and L2 as tools for learning and as competences in their own right (Kasper and Rose 2002: 33). Students learning through their L1 need support in order to master academic language, which as Bourdieu and Passeron (1994: 8) point out 'is nobody's mother tongue'. Academic language includes the language needed for learning and imparting new skills and knowledge, and for discussing abstract ideas and building conceptual understanding (Chamot and O'Malley 1996). It is much more complex and its corpus is over ten times that of social language (Hu and Nation 2000). Moreover, as a command of academic language underpins student achievement it is particularly important that this language be taught explicitly (Murphy 2016). In bilingual education, one is faced with the particular difficulty of helping students with limited L2 language skills to learn both academic language and use that language to think about and analyse complex content concepts.

Taking a language-sensitive approach to teaching content subjects is considered a hallmark of bilingual education. Many researchers and practitioners working in bilingual education or with students who are not yet proficient in the language of instruction call for the concurrent and integrated teaching of content and language (Echevarria et al. 2008; Gibbons 2009; National Academies of Sciences, Engineering and Medicine 2017). The principle that all content teachers also assume responsibility for language teaching is also at the core of the Content and Language Integrated Learning (CLIL) movement, a frequently used term to describe diverse types of additive bilingual education (cf. Genesee and Hamayan 2016). In addition, in education systems teaching primarily through a national or regional language, the languages across the curriculum movement, the start of which Parker (1985) dates to 1966, essentially argues for the use of a language-sensitive approach to teaching. The seminal *A Language for Life* report maintains that language plays a central role in mediating learning and therefore, that every content teacher is also a language teacher (Bullock 1975). The report's primary conclusion is that secondary schools should foster language learning across the curriculum. These principles continue to be held in high esteem by experts in the field, the curricula of several nations and supranational bodies such the Council of Europe (Vollmer 2006).

The consequences of not taking a language-sensitive approach can be significant. Considerable evidence suggests that if students are not fully proficient in the language of instruction and educators do not support the learning of academic language, and if oral and written language instruction is not integrated into content classes, content learning and academic achievement can in general suffer (National Academies of Sciences, Engineering and Medicine 2017). In addition, Johnstone (2002) points to a tendency for bilingual education students' L2 language development to reach a plateau where certain gender, syntax and morphological errors become fossilised, and the students' language use may not be appropriate to context (e.g. they may use an informal register in a formal context). This is a level of language where students can communicate with relative ease, but where their language usage is still far removed from that of a native speaker. In these cases, the students and the teachers appear to be more motivated by content learning than language learning. Lyster (2007: 42–43) points out that 'language features learned in isolated grammar lessons may be remembered [...] during a grammar test,' but that they are less likely to be retrieved during content classes. To prevent fossilisation of errors Lyster (ibid.) proposes maintaining a dual focus on content and language by counterbalancing content-based and form-focused instruction and doing this across the curriculum.

There is some evidence that European schools' students have been able to achieve results that are superior to Canadian bilingual education students' results, and this sometimes in shorter periods of time (Genesee and Baetens Beardsmore 2013). Housen (2002a, b) studied the L2 achievements of European schools' students in three different countries. He reported that despite having little out-of-school support for learning the

L2, students produced 'grammatically accurate and lexically precise sustained discourse in an L2' (Housen 2002a: 213). Housen stressed that these levels were only achieved at the end of secondary schooling.

As we have already suggested, a concrete manifestation of a language-sensitive approach to teaching content subjects would, at the very least, be reflected in curriculum documents through the inclusion of language objectives. Without language objectives, it is difficult for teachers to plan for student learning. Clear intended language objectives not only provide a focus for planning lessons, but they also facilitate course development and the choice, adaptation and/or creation of learning resources.

Moreover, clear and concise language objectives explain to learners what is expected of them. If language-learning expectations are not clear, it is difficult for a student to see his or her own language-learning path, to assess progress and to plan for further language learning. Objectives are considered fundamental to building and maintaining learner motivation (Gardner 1985; MacIntyre 2002). They have the potential of supporting learner autonomy. Legenhausen (2009) asserts that in a classroom fostering autonomy students participate in the planning. They negotiate decisions pertaining to the learning process for which they will be held accountable. They do their planned work undertaking the necessary research. Finally, they evaluate both the learning process and their progress. Language objectives are a key mechanism for students and teachers in managing the language learning process in a thoughtful and explicit manner.

Content objectives all involve language; however, the emphasis in those objectives is primarily on content learning. Language objectives primarily focus on one or more of the following four aspects of language (Mehisto and Ting 2017):

Language Awareness These objectives focus on the use of academic *versus* social language and on grammatical conventions. Students are able to:

- maintain a consistent and precise use of terminology and other scientific vocabulary throughout a written text;
- organise a written report under the following headings: purpose of the experiment, hypothesis, variables and constants, equipment, method, findings and conclusions.

- use correctly the phraseology and terminology for a given unit found in the class language bank;
- recognise and defend against the use of emotional language; and
- identify the language of subjectivity.

Communicative Competence These objectives focus on the nature of communication such as whether students are using short answers *versus* a well-developed line of reasoning and the richness or paucity of language being used. Students are able to:

- support their opinion with a two-point explanation;
- partake actively in classroom discussions and group work using the L2;
- manage their voice (volume, intonation, enunciation, tone) when making a presentation;
- use a rich diversity of language to elaborate and clarify;
- create detailed and easy-to-follow instructions for conducting diverse tasks (e.g. an experiment, a line of enquiry).

Language Learning Skills These objectives are focussed on developing meta-cognitive and meta-linguistic awareness that allow students to take better charge of their own language learning. Students are able to:

- read a text for different purposes (e.g. consistent flow of ideas, grammar, spelling);
- use an L2 thesaurus to enrich language use in their written work;
- skim long (and complex) texts to decide whether a source is suitable for further study;
- make research notes in an organised fashion that allows them later to find relevant information quickly;
- (a) create successive draft versions of a text; (b) test the intelligibility of their text based on the reactions of others; and, (c) use what they have learned to correct and improve their text.

Cross-Cultural Communication These objectives focus on the previously discussed construct of intercultural competence with a particular focus on knowledge, skills, attitudes and values. Students are able to:

- use formulae of politeness appropriately;
- suspend immediate judgement whilst analysing unfamiliar situations when reading about people from X culture
- compare their own non-verbal communication practices with those of people from other cultures;
- and demonstrate deep order perspective-taking (based on Candelier et al. 2012; Deardorff 2013).

Just as is the case with making a shift to content-based instruction in language classes, taking a language-sensitive approach to the teaching of content subjects implies a major shift in practice. As we have discussed above, a shift to language-sensitive teaching in content subjects will have implications for curriculum and course development, teaching and learning practices, teacher cooperation, assessment, professional development plans, and for management and leadership practices.

Languages of Instruction

In a bi-/tri-/multilingual education environment that seeks to foster additive bi-/tri-/multilingualism, the language used to teach any given subject, as long as each language is used to teach some high status subjects, is a secondary issue when compared with the quality of teaching and learning practices. There is no subject that one could say with absolute certainty that it should be taught through the L2 or L3. Every subject being taught through the L2 or L3 could be considered as having its own challenges and benefits. In general, a deciding factor of the language of instruction is the availability of teachers (Ruiz de Zarobe 2015). From the students' perspective, their preferences for a given language of instruction may be motivated by where and in which language they wish to undertake their post-secondary studies.

The core principles of ensuring that as many students as possible receive their education in their L1, that all pupils undergo the study of some subjects in their L2, and that all students study an L3, and that those students without language sections at least receive language classes in their L1 have served the European schools well. These structural arrangements are a manifestation of the education system's and its stakeholders' values; their respect for mother tongue, multilingualism and multiculturalism. Any attempt to use arguments such as the generally higher than average academic achievement of SWALS to reduce the number of language sections would strike at the heart of the European schools' core values.

However, despite the general high level of achievement of SWALS, there are two primary areas of concern: the extra challenges these students face especially when having to study subjects through their L3 or L4, and how well prepared they will be to undertake post-secondary studies in their L1. SWALS can find themselves in mixed language groups (i.e. in Art, ICT, Music and Physical Education). In these circumstances decisions about pedagogy and which language or languages of instruction will be used for teaching, learning and assessment take on a particular importance. It is possible for European schools' students in S1 to find themselves in a subject such as ICT that is being taught in their L3 whilst they are only beginning to study their L3. This begs the question as to what extent students' needs vary in mixed language groups due to language knowledge, and how learning is being scaffolded and differentiated individually for students who are learning through their L2 or L3. We are unaware of European schools being provided with any direction other than having English, French or German being prescribed as a medium of instruction for these subjects. In addition, we are unaware of how European schools' teachers, teaching mixed language groups, are trained, and what expectations are placed on them regarding differentiation and 'multilingual education'. Finally, should SWALS wish to return to their country of origin to undertake post-secondary education, it is debatable whether their L1 language classes alone would allow these students to develop sufficient proficiency in the academic registers of their L1 to be prepared for continued study through that language.

One of several possible ways of helping to address the language needs of SWALS when they are studying subjects through their L3 or L4, which can have the added benefit of helping them to prepare for post-secondary studies, is to use 'translanguaging' in one and the same subject (Williams 1996). Translanguaging involves speaking, listening, reading and/or writing about a topic in one language, and then speaking or writing about it in another. In translanguaging 'both languages are used in an integrated and coherent way to organise and mediate learning' (Baker 2011). The focus of translanguaging is on meaning making and gaining a deeper understanding of subject matter content through two languages. It avoids any overuse of the L1 in classes taught through another language that might in the long-term undermine the learning of the additional language. Translanguaging can also be used as a strategy for having students who are studying most of their subjects through an L2, to gain exposure to L1 academic language. On a practical level, translanguaging includes activities such as having students: draft an outline of a report in their L1, get feedback from the teacher in their L2, and write the report in their L2; conduct an enquiry that requires the use of L1 and L2 sources when doing their research; and, analyse three texts in two (or if possible three) different languages about an historical event (e.g. three stakeholder perspectives) and then compare that analysis with what they read in a highly respected foreign press report that seeks to offer a balanced overview.

The rising popularity of translanguaging signals a shift from the previously held view that it is important in bilingual education to keep the two languages apart (Heugh 2016). Teachers teaching through the L2 were expected to teach only through the L2. However, in practice teachers may have been more flexible, often using as much L2 as possible and as little L1 as necessary (Little and Boynton 2004). Currently, it is no longer suggested that teachers teaching through the L2 should never or almost never use the students' L1. There is an increasing recognition that languages are interdependent (Cummins 2000) and that it is normal to mix languages when speaking in informal contexts, but essential to be able to separate languages when producing written academic work (Heugh 2016).

Although more research is required on the matter, initial indications are that translanguaging may: lead to deeper conceptual understanding of a topic; help students to better encode learning in memory; and allow for easier retrieval of learning from memory (Baker 2011). Similarly, Genesee and Hamayan (2016: 109) suggest that: 'cross-linguistic connections create meaning; learning in and about one language supports learning in and about another language; making the two languages an integral part of lessons reflects the value and high status of both languages; and discussing concepts in more than one language helps to better encode knowledge in the brain for later use.'

Despite the success of the European Schools' teaching of and through languages, their lack of an overall language policy, language objectives in content curricula and a breakdown of intercultural competences, as well as their seemingly content-light language curricula, all imply that the European Schools are under-utilising policy prescriptions and powerful pedagogical principles to drive language and intercultural learning. Moreover, existing European schools' key documents include little or no discussion of or practical guidelines about how summative and formative assessment in a bilingual school fostering multilingualism is unique or different to assessment in a primarily monolingual education context. This is reinforced by the fact that only fleeting mention is made to teaching methodology or other aspects of pedagogy in the minutes of the Working Group 'Organisation of studies in the secondary cycle' or in the Proposal of the 'Organisation of studies in the secondary cycle' Working Group or in our face-to-face meetings during the research project. In addition, whilst the European Schools are showing clear concern for students in particular with regards to the failure and drop out rates, the near absence of discussion about the quality of teaching in relation to dropout rates seems to covertly place the responsibility for these rates on the current organisation of studies and students, but not on teaching. There is currently a need to accord the quality of teaching and in particular student learning considerably more attention on policy and meeting agendas. This could help ensure that the European Schools are first and foremost a learning-powered institution that also understands and takes into account the specificities of bilingual education. In the next chapter, we examine issues of social selection, sorting and segregation in relation to educational practices within the European schools.

Open Access This chapter is licensed under the terms of the Creative Commons Attribution 4.0 International License (http://creativecommons.org/licenses/by/4.0/), which permits use, sharing, adaptation, distribution and reproduction in any medium or format, as long as you give appropriate credit to the original author(s) and the source, provide a link to the Creative Commons license and indicate if changes were made.

The images or other third party material in this chapter are included in the chapter's Creative Commons license, unless indicated otherwise in a credit line to the material. If material is not included in the chapter's Creative Commons license and your intended use is not permitted by statutory regulation or exceeds the permitted use, you will need to obtain permission directly from the copyright holder.

4

A United and Thriving Europe? A Sociology of the European Schools

Over the past sixty years European society has seen dramatic changes. Yet even though the European Schools System has been described as a 'social and cultural laboratory', it has changed comparatively little during that time. What we do see, however, is a gradual process of social and cultural assimilation that has been increasingly put under pressure as a result of EU expansion and new social imperatives. This chapter draws on existing literature as well as new empirical material to analyse key themes that arise as a consequence of such tensions. The issues of social selection, sorting and segregation are considered in relation to educational practices within the European Schools as well as their relationships with local, national and international neighbours. Complex forms of citizenship in the European Schools are defined and analysed, and their interrelationships mapped out. In this way we present an original framework for defining the enduring characteristics of the European schools, as well as those that may need adapting for the future. This also has relevance for the evolution of international schools that are not part of the European Schools System.

Ideological Roots of the European Schools

As discussed earlier in this book, the European schools were designed initially as an inter-governmental education system with highly distinctive characteristics (Savvides 2006a, b, c; Carlos 2012). They were designed to be an important part of the European project. As such, the European schools were firmly grounded in an ideology of a 'united and thriving Europe' (Hayden and Thompson 1997). There was a further agenda, however, as education delivered in this manner was quite deliberately seen by its founders as a site for engineering cultural integration (Theiler 1999). In this way, it was thought, the European schools initiative would be able to develop an innovative international model grounded in mutual co-operation. Carlos (2012: 488) describes this as 'an imagining of Europe, in its earliest and simplest form'.

The European Schools System is based on the idea of three pillars (Shore and Baratieri 2005):

1. Education should be in the official languages of the European member states.
2. The syllabus and timetables should align to that of the various European member states, allowing for flexible entry and leaving points as students go backwards and forwards to their home countries, with no educational disadvantage. This includes the provision of the European Baccalaureate as an alternative to national pre-university entry qualifications.
3. The promotion of cultural exchange.

Mechanisms for this form of European integration included the construction of a history and geography curriculum that attempted to transcend borders, with instruction from multiple vantage points and national positions. For example, an early EC newsletter for a US readership describes how the European Schools were supplied with specialist maps of Europe, including roads, railways and major agricultural and industrial areas, putting them into a European rather than national context (European Community 1964). Another curriculum tool that was deployed was privileged access to native speakers of other languages, which led to enhanced opportunities for plurilingual education. Both tools contributed to a polydirectional and polycultural version of pedagogic reform, rather than one grounded in existing systems that predominated in any particular country (Rydenvald 2015). The combination of these social, cultural and linguistic factors also contributed to high academic standards, with the apparent bonus of creating what we might describe as 'mini citizens of Europe', and through this, promoting ideals of European unity. Indeed some have described the European Schools as a pedagogical mini-Europe (Haas 2004).

The system was always intended to expand indefinitely in response to the need and desire of citizens. Early on there was recognition that there could be other European schools in member states in the future (Jonckers 2000). By 2004, twelve had been established in total, but the system was reported to be in crisis due to two main factors. The first factor was overcrowding after European expansion into Eastern Europe. The second was the advent of Estonians, Latvians, Lithuanians, Czechs and Slovaks, amongst others, who wanted to be taught in English or French and not in their mother tongue, because they regarded English or French as 'more useful' as primary languages in terms of their children's education. This put an additional strain on teachers in the European schools, as they were being required to fulfil new pedagogical roles that were never anticipated by the original founders of the system, such as teaching non-native speakers in L1 (native tongue) classes (Kinstler 2015).

In spite of apparent difficulties in the practical aspects of delivery, there has been extensive demand amongst parents for the European schools model, even if they do not have a professional connection to the European Commission. While this group of parents is entitled to apply for school places on behalf of their children, in most of the European schools it is likely to be extremely difficult to find a place in view of the general problems of overcrowding that is placing a strain on most of the original European schools. One solution to this supply and demand problem has been to found accredited schools (Category II schools receive funding from Brussels and prioritise the children of Commission employees, unlike Category III schools) or Category III schools, which are not subject to the same legal, administrative and financial arrangements as their European Commission cousins, and which do not form part of the intergovernmental system of education, but which nevertheless meet the same pedagogical standards (Board of Governors 2013). This 2009 expansion indicates growing appetite for the European Schools model amongst parents and students, beyond Brussels and indeed the European Commission.

The Impact of Maastricht

In addition to the expansion of Europe in 2004, another turning point for the European Schools pedagogical model had been the Maastricht treaty of 1992, when the European Community became the European Union. The Treaty was designed to bring about significantly closer involvement amongst Member States in the areas of matters such as foreign policy, military, criminal justice, and the judiciary. Article 127 of the Maastricht Treaty lays out its position on education:

> The Community shall contribute to the development of quality education by encouraging co-operation between Member States and, if necessary, by supporting and supplementing their action, while fully respecting the responsibility of the Member States for the content of teaching and the organisation of education systems and their cultural and linguistic diversity.

There were some reservations within some member states about the desire for what had been termed 'ever-closer union amongst the peoples of Europe', a term dating from the earliest days of the European Community in 1957 and at the time, meant in a different context relating to mutual peace and co-operation (European Community 1957). This, combined with low turnouts in EU elections, led to the beginning of a potential lack of legitimacy for the EU (Savvides, op. cit. 2006a, b, c). There was also a perceived lack of a sense of European loyalty or identity (Garcia and Wallace 1993, cited in Savvides, ibid.). In turn, this also linked to a lack of electoral will for a proposed European Union constitution, especially in France and the Netherlands. From this it appears that the project of cultural integration was starting to falter, something that in time would also impact on the European schools, and which is discussed later in this chapter.

It was in the context of this that the post-1993 Directorate General XXII for Education, Training and Youth was established. Under the auspices of the Socrates programme, the Directorate has concentrated on programmes such as:

1. ERASMUS (European Community Action Scheme for the Mobility of University Students, originally established in 1987)
2. LINGUA (a language teaching and learning programme, originally established in 1989)
3. COMENIUS (a primary and secondary education development programme aimed at encouraging school partnerships, established in 1994)
4. GRUNDTVIG (an adult education and lifelong learning development programme, established in 2007)

While these programmes clearly have education at their core, they are essentially about contact amongst and between EU member states and not about directly inserting distinctively European content into curriculum. This has been avoided because of what is seen as a nation state problem, with the principle of subsidiarity, meaning that individual countries wanted to retain control and direction of their educational systems. This is in spite of the apparent identification in the 1973 Janne report of 'an irreversible recognition of an educational dimension of Europe and the irreversible initial movement towards an education policy at European Community level' (Janne 1973: 10), and attempts within the Lisbon Treaty of 2007 to achieve greater levels of educational harmonisation across Europe, for example, with regard to qualifications. The absence of this kind of shared European curriculum and assessment process has meant that member states have never had access to the kind of tool that would allow them to buy in completely to the idea of cross-European educational unity. This both reflects the educational *zeitgeist* across Europe, resistant to a perceived loss of national independence, whilst at the same time presenting a significant area of tension in terms of future collaborative development amongst different countries.

Another area of tension is symbolised by the relationship between official versus unofficial EU languages. Within the European Community, and later the European Union, the 'vehicular' languages of French,

German and English have been given privileged status, illustrating the cultural hegemony of the core member states (Shore and Baratieri 2005), whereas languages such as Maltese, Irish, Basque, Catalan and Welsh have been seen as less important (indeed Welsh, Basque and Catalan do not appear at all as official EU languages, even today, despite the fact that two of these languages are widely spoken in more than one country). To understand why this concept of the vehicular language links to an inherent problem of legitimacy, we need to consider the concept of folk versus elite bilingualism, as discussed in Bulwer (1995). Folk bilingualism (for example Maltese, Irish, Basque, Catalan and Welsh, as listed above) is not seem as an active choice, but instead something that has grown out of the domestic situation of a child. In this way such languages are minoritised and marginalised (Nic Craith 2006). Elite bilingualism, on the other hand, is potentially seen as more progressive and associated with modernity (ibid.). It has a more international mindset and has usually come about as a result of a conscious decision to study socially and economically useful languages with the potential for use in a professional context later in life. These are the reasons invoked by Eastern European parents for accessing L1 provision in English, French or German even though their child's native tongue may in fact be Estonian, Czech, or Slovak. Meanwhile languages such as Maltese, Irish, Basque, Catalan and Welsh (or indeed Estonian, Czech or Slovak) continue to be implicitly treated as 'folk' languages (even where they are nationally recognised in their own member states as official languages) and not resourced to the same degree. While there may be sound practical and financial reasons underpinning this decision, the consequence is a two-tier structure that appears remote from the everyday concerns of millions of linguistically diverse European citizens in other regions. Even within the EU itself, of the three 'vehicular' languages, it is English and French that largely dominate, possibly on the basis that they are historically used as diplomatic languages, and in the case of English, possibly also because more twenty-first century technical, scientific and computing terms exist within it than most other languages (ibid.)

In Chap. 3 we discussed the technical aspects of language education and the European schools in considerable depth, but it is also necessary to touch on it to a certain extent here. Even though the principle of learning other languages is securely embedded within the European schools' pedagogical structures and philosophy, there is little if any scientific evidence for their current approach to languages, where children study them in a semi-osmotic way in class (Gray 2003; Leaton Gray et al. 2015). This is because much of the teaching is not sufficiently explicit. Consequently the standards required in terms of learning different languages are unclear. The current practice of examining many subjects orally as well as in written form contributes to a lack of clarity surrounding requirements, as it means it is unclear whether final examinations are assessing the subject knowledge or the language of examination. Indeed, this is a major concern, which has led to the reform of the European Baccalaureate final diploma (ibid.).

Despite these difficulties of tracking and assessing linguistic progress out of context, the impact of 'peer talk' in language learning in European schools may be profound (Baetens Beardsmore and Kohls 1988). Another advantage of the natural ebb and flow of many languages within the European schools is that structures are orientated around horizontal tolerance of different cultures and language speakers, promoting the ability to be critically reflective on the nature of one's own culture and language, as well as the way they impact on others, and promoting a more healthy sense of citizenship (Starkey, op. cit.). Nevertheless, while this is laudable, languages are still taken for granted in the current system to a certain extent, and one criticism might be that language instruction perhaps doesn't go far enough in terms of deeper integration. This leads once again to the problems of legitimacy first seen in the Maastricht outcome (Theiler 1999) and reminds us that the European dimension in such schooling can be relatively vague, with an occasional lack of curricular coherence (ibid.). Theiler predicted the wider demise of the EU on grounds of problems such as these, and he was not alone in anticipating Europe's current difficulties. There are also clues evident in an important quotation in the work of Savvides, by a teacher interviewee who probably did not know how prescient he or she was being:

> I do not feel I'm really European because I don't know what it means … so far for me the EU is not linked to people. It's a financial world, a political world … an economic world, it's not a people world. (Savvides 2006c: 125)

Here we see an identity issue being raised; people in the system have a sense of being involved with European integration in some way, but they don't necessarily have a feeling of what it might mean to be a 'European'. The personal and the political seem to be divided.

Social Selection, Sorting and Segregation

Novel patterns of system governance have resulted in administrative and diplomatic complexity within the European Union, and this is reflected within the European Schools. There are multiple power bases, which engage in complex interactions both within and across different networks, both vertically and horizontally. Ansell (2000) terms this 'networked polity', although he refers to the term at a regional level rather than an institutional one, as in this case. Hence we see a complex assemblage of actors (as described by Carlos, op. cit.) with multiple stakeholders, for example: students, parents, Interparents (Parent Association), teachers, directors, Joint Teaching Committee, Board of Governors, Office of the Secretary General of the European Schools, Joint Board of Inspectors, working groups, and the European Commission.

Within this structure, there are continuous negotiations taking place amongst and across groups, through the endeavours of the various working parties in place at any particular time, a practice explained in considerable depth by Carlos (*ibid.*). She describes a cyclical model that involves policy proposals flowing from one board to another, underpinned by new forms of meaning enacted at different stages. This negotiation and renegotiation leads to somewhat blurred boundaries, with the regular and routine grouping and regrouping of power bases and rules. To an extent, such practices are unsurprising, and simply indicative of the usual power struggles routinely inherent within any form of policymaking, where lobbying and bargaining are embedded within everyday interactions. Yet, the particular complexity of this model, and its hierarchical structure, can result in parents being excluded from voting rights, particular in the case of financial matters, representing a form of stakeholder segregation. The next part of the chapter deals with other forms of social selection, sorting and segregation, with particular reference to the impact on students.

Selection

The European Schools System is meant to be comprehensive, which resembles the English system of secondary school, but incorporates some aspects of the French and German systems, such as a broad curriculum throughout, with only limited subject selection. Another characteristic of the European Schools System is the use of *retention*, where a student is kept down a year if he or she is seen as not meeting the usual standards of the existing year cohort. Educationally speaking, this type of intervention is unlikely to be effective and can even be seen as a problem (cf. Hattie 2008; Martinez et al. 2015). In the case of the European Schools, some children who don't fit with the system are held back for multiple years and eventually encouraged to leave the European schooling system altogether if matters aren't resolved.

As far as students are concerned, retention may simply be a consequence of being in the wrong European school or language section at the wrong time, something that has little if anything to do with innate student ability. This is clearly evident within retention rates, which differ considerably across the different schools and countries. For example, if we examine the retention data for the primary sector (P1–P6), for 2010 to 2012 (the latest available literature freely available to the authors), we see that it is 0.1% to 1.2% in Culham, UK, where this is not regarded as a common educational practice, and the highest is 3.1% to 3.9% in Luxembourg 1, and 2.5% to 5.3% in Mol, examples of where retention may be more closely aligned to prior teacher expectations. Mean rates were 2.2% to 2.7% across all European Schools P1–P6 for this period. As the rates differ so much, to the sociologist's eye, it seems less likely to be caused by student unsuitability, and more likely to be a consequence of regional cultural practices and expectations.

The practice of retention can have negative consequences. Sociologically speaking, retention with the year group below may well bring with it a potential sense of *anomie* (alienation) on the grounds that one doesn't fit. In this way, the European schools' upper secondary triaging of students into an 'in-group' (who can cope with the work) and an 'out-group' (who can't cope with the work) amounts to clear evidence of social selection, with unintended outcomes when students leave for academic reasons (as opposed to family relocation for work, for example). This is very different from the inclusive, comprehensive model of schooling envisaged by its founders. In our 2014–2015 research into the upper secondary curriculum, we spoke to several students who had survived the sudden conceptual shift required by the mathematics and science curricula at S4–S5 level (age 14–15), something that is said to be a known phenomenon within the European schools. Their view on leavers was that 'those students did not work hard enough' and 'we don't have anything to do with those students now, we are not in touch', indicating a kind of social ostracism once a student had left, because the student concerned had not made the grade academically (or indeed never fitted in at all).

This social selection also has an effect on the perceived standard of the European Schools System by outsiders. This is because in educational attainment terms, the success of these schools at upper secondary level is being measured by the success of those who have survived what can be a challenging, and even somewhat academically harsh, system for certain types of child, effectively selecting them at the age of around 15. From our discussions with European schools inspectors during 2014–2015, we found that this may present problems for late developers, those with special educational needs, and those who start in the system late with relatively weak L2 (second language) and L3 (third language) skills. Another category of student that might experience difficulties are those who are more vocationally inclined, as there is virtually no provision in this regard. For them, the system can be a very difficult one. Therefore what we may be seeing here is less a kind of social selection, and more a kind of inadvertent segregation, linked to how familiar and established families are within the European Schools System and the Commission itself, and how closely they fit with existing social groupings there. Shore and Baratieri have described this group as:

> A social class that does not need to worry about obtaining a specific job on leaving secondary school and, perhaps, confirms their status as a highly adaptable and mobile group in the top ranks of Europe's elite. (Shore and Baratieri 2005: 36)

Social distance, leading to a child leaving a European School for reasons other than parental employment, may simply be a manifestation of the kinds of class-based problems we see in segregated schooling systems elsewhere, where belonging to a higher social class (or in this case a class of elite bilinguals) can be educationally advantageous (cf. Jenkins et al. 2006; Ball 2006). We therefore now turn to the issue of social segregation.

Segregation

European schools are often described as being more like 'company schools', providing a facility for a clearly defined social group, in this case certain types of employees. This is because they have very strict admissions rules, as follows (Fig. 4.1):

- **Category I**: Students who have to be admitted by the European Schools. These students are exempt from school fees.
- **Category II**: Students covered by individual agreements or decisions, each entailing specific rights and obligations for the students concerned, particularly as regards school fees.
- **Category III**: Students who do not belong to categories I and II. These students would be admitted to the European Schools in so far as places are available, in accordance with an order of priority listed here. The ordinary school fees fixed by the Board of Governors would be payable for these students.

Category I
The children of staff in the service of the Community institutions and of the organisations listed below [1] employed directly and continuously for a minimum period of one year.

1. Members of the Community Institutions
2. Officials covered by the Staff Regulations of Officials of the European Communities [*]
3. Staff covered by the Conditions of Employment of other Servants of the European Communities [*]

4. Persons with a directly binding contract of employment, governed by private law, with the Community Institutions
5. National experts seconded to Community Institutions
6. Employees of the E.I.B.
7. Staff of any Community organisation set up by an act of the Community Institutions and staff in the service of other organisations recognised by the Board of Governors
8. UKAEA staff seconded to the JET project at Culham
9. Staff of the European Investment Fund's Secretariat
10. National officials attached to the Permanent Representations of the Member States to the European Communities, with the exception of staff recruited locally
11. Teaching staff and the administrative and ancillary staff of the European Schools and of the Office of the Representative of the Board of Governors
12. Staff covered by the Service Regulations of the EPO in Munich.

The special conditions governing the admission of the children referred to in points 1 to 11 to the Munich School and those for the children referred to in point 12 to the other Schools are determined by the Board of Governors.

Category II
Students covered by individual agreements or decisions, each entailing specific rights and obligations for the students concerned.

Category III
The order in which the following students are listed is the order of priority for admission purposes:

(a) Children of national officials seconded to diplomatic representations, to the NATO Representation and to the Consulates of the Member States (with the exception of locally recruited staff);

(b) Children of members of the diplomatic service returning to their home country in which a European School is situated and where they can only be integrated into the national education system in place with great difficulty on account of the latter's special features;
(c) Children of national officials of the Permanent Representations of non-member States to the European Communities (with the exception of locally recruited staff);
(d) Children of staff with diplomatic status, posted in Brussels or in Luxembourg, belonging to non-member countries which signed the Lomé Convention;
(e) Other officials posted abroad, in all the Schools;
(f) Others: priority will be given to students whose mother tongue or language of previous education is not a language of tuition in the national education system.

Please Note the Admission Regulations for Category III Students

a) Decisions on admissions in category III, as allowed by the regulations, are taken by the Director, in accordance with the provisions of Article 8 of the General Rules of the European Schools.

In admitting such students, the Director must ensure that enough places are kept free in each class to allow a reasonable number of children coming into categories I and II to be admitted during the year without this leading to a class having to be divided.

b) No category III student may be admitted to a class which already has 24 students at the beginning of the school year.
c) See also the "Policy on Enrolment in the European Schools in Brussels" and the "Admission Criteria of the European School, Munich".

Admission of Children of Assistance of Members of the European Parliament

1. Admission of the children of accredited parliamentary assistants
The Board of Governors confirmed that the children of accredited parliamentary assistants come under Category I for purposes of access to the European Schools.
2. Admission of the children of local assistants of Members of the European Parliament
The Board of Governors decided that the children of local assistants of Members of the European Parliament are classified in Category III for purposes of admission to the European Schools.

(Source: Office of the Secretary General of the European Schools 2017)
https://www.eursc.eu/en/European-Schools/enrolments/admission

Fig. 4.1 Terms and conditions of admission

The argument for describing them as 'company schools' as opposed to 'international schools' has some grounds. Despite the fact that children from many different nationalities attend them, looking at the admissions rules, they use a distinctive model that is not as straightforward or inclusive as a normal international school. By its very nature and location, the model and the curriculum exclude many non-Europeans, as they will not be eligible for many diplomatic or civil service posts in European member states or within the Commission itself. In turn, the curriculum itself specifically privileges European perspectives over global ones, for example through the incorporation of 'European Hours'. This comes at the expense of an international perspective in the truly global sense, and potentially risks promoting what Starkey describes as a form of 'Eurocentric cultural superiority' (Starkey 2012).

Another issue in terms of segregation is that European schools also have very little to do with their immediate local communities, as a rule, in that they are not embedded within local educational authorities and they generally don't share many facilities or resources with other local schools. In this way, the somewhat isolationist nature of EU Schools belies their supposed social liberal philosophy in some respects, as students may be standing side by side with each other but certainly not socially adjacent to their geographical neighbours. Finally, if we look at the admissions rules for Category 3 students, the category for those families who do not have a diplomatic or employment connection with the European Schools, fees can range from around 3500 Euros a year to around 6800 Euros a year depending on the phase of education. For many local families on a national average wage or below, such fees may be prohibitive, particularly if they have more than one child of school age. Consequently students in the European schools are schooled apart from other students in the local area, as well as those who can't afford fees or who are not members of the European diplomatic, scientific and political 'family'. Their system is segregated on multiple levels, and has been accused of encouraging elitism through this, as well as through an apparent lack of accountability (Oostlander 1993).

A different kind of system segregation is encountered by some European schools' teachers in relation to the fact that various forms of national law can come into direct conflict with European law when it comes to the terms and conditions for their employment. The principle of subsidiarity means that the European Union has no hard powers to determine education or teacher employment policy across all its 28 member states. Instead it relies on negotiation, which sometimes can be problematic. For example, there has been conflict between UK national employment law and European law in relation to the standard nine-year contracts used for teacher secondments from the UK education system to the European Schools System. The intention of these limited-term contracts is to ensure that teachers stay in touch with developments in their national systems. This is a very different type of employment from an international school, where teachers might be on indefinite contracts. It has come about because in many countries in Europe, teachers are directly employed by the State, and allocated to a particular school or region, meaning that, if an EU schools' secondment ends, they can simply go back to their home country and be relatively easily redeployed. In the UK, teachers are employed not by the State, but an individual school, meaning that when an EU schools' secondment finishes after nine years, the teacher is made redundant and accrued employment rights are lost. This places a UK teacher at a disadvantage compared to, say, a French,

German or Greek teacher, where their Governments will ensure (and indeed underwrite) the teacher's continuing employment (Schmalenbach 2010). Therefore, for a UK-funded teacher, their experience of the system amounts to a form of segregation in a wholly different model from the national system they are expected to return to. This is diametrically opposed to the original intention of the nine-year secondment model, and a problem to which the EU Commission (or the UK for that matter) has been able to offer little in the way of a useful solution.

Another symptom of segregation is that European Schools can seem disconnected from the wider community, as touched on previously (Hayden and Thompson 1997). This happens on two levels. In geographical terms, it would be possible to stand in a European school building, and not know which country you were in unless you knew already, for example. This represents an unusual form of Eurocentrism in which the culture of European schools overrides national cultures. The second level is that this inherent cultural hegemony also overrides wider European ones outside the immediate European employee community (ibid.). In practical terms, this means that although you may live physically next door to a European school (and indeed be funding such schools indirectly via taxation), you will find yourself paying school fees to attend a European school as outlined earlier in the chapter, if a place is available for students in your category of applicant (and this is unlikely). It also applies to those closely connected with the European Union but not actually employed by the Commission, such as local journalists, lobbyists, and sub-contractors. They also find themselves with inferior access to European schools, even though it could be argued that they are an essential part of the Brussels political machinery. In this way, segregation has taken a number of forms, just as it has for teachers and students. As Stacul et al. (2006) argue, the pedagogical laboratory of the European School has resulted in exclusive institutions that try to dissolve the boundaries of national cultures at the same times as reinforcing class boundaries. This is because they are not designed to include a mass public.

Sorting

The frequently stated desire amongst EU Schools, parents and students for an education that focuses on speaking multiple languages can be seen as a kind of social sorting, in which families seek membership of a specific social group, in this case a caste of 'elite bilinguals'. As explained earlier in the chapter, these are people who have learnt additional languages out of choice as an enhancement to their social, cultural and intellectual capital, as opposed to 'folk bilinguals' who have learnt a second language in addition to their national one, or as a result of immigration. This desire for elite bilingualism has created a number of problems within the European schooling system in recent years. For example, the UK has until recently found itself in the position of 'over-seconding' UK-funded state school teachers to European schools (Interparents 2013). This is because of the rise in the importance of ESOL (English as a Second or Other Language) internationally, leading to the predominance of English as the chosen L2 (second language) within the European schools. Occasionally non-native speakers of English have also requested to be allocated to English mother tongue classes as well. Initially the UK Government routinely provided the majority of native speakers required to underpin such provision, but increasingly with greater numbers of non-UK students wanting such provision and fewer UK students actually attending the European schools, the UK Government argued that they were funding provision disproportionately and this represented a form of over-secondment (Bulwer, op. cit.; Interparents, op. cit.). Presumably the recent UK referendum and Brexit vote will make the provision of L2 (second language) English even more problematic in years to come, as the UK Government withdraws completely from provision, leaving English provision in the hands of the Irish and Maltese Governments.

Students are also sorted on the basis of mother tongue. It is often stated that many of the larger European schools are effectively 'schools within schools' on account of the number of different language sections that a school contains. When we visited Brussels III during the academic year 2014–2015, for example, we found there to be seven language sections in total: Czech, German, Greek, English, Spanish, French and Dutch. In a language section, students are taught in the mother tongue of that section. It is also possible to be a student without a languages section (known as SWALS), educated in a language section of his or her choosing. The existence of language sections leads to another unusual and somewhat contradictory phenomenon within the European schools, whereby the central model, whilst at the same time being reinforced by the mother tongue groupings of students, erodes nationalism.

The practicalities underpinning educational delivery in such a complex, plurilingual context contribute to this. Over the years there have been various attempts to produce teaching materials in different languages. These were usually widely distributed but not always properly evaluated (Theiler, op. cit.). The outcome was that special European schools' textbooks were not always considered appropriate by teachers (Savvides 2006b), who instead developed their own teaching materials. This led in some circumstances to a lack of collaboration amongst some European schools' teachers from different nationalities, and in turn a somewhat atomised form of professional identity for some teachers (ibid.) Similarly, student identity can be somewhat atomised as well. It is clear that there is usually unqualified approval of students trying to speak other languages, but this does not automatically lead to high levels of competence in non-native tongues, or deep integration. This is because the pedagogy of language instruction within the European schools is not always sufficiently well-structured (Baetens Beardsmore and Kohls 1988). This can lead to limitations to the linguistic ability of some students, where they can speak enough of an additional language to 'get by', but not necessarily a great deal more (Shore and Baratieri 2005).

A further issue peculiar to the European schools is that while multiple languages are welcomed, relatively few sociocultural demands are put on students in terms of integration due to the existence of language sections as 'mini schools' (Bulwer 1995). That having been said, it would be very wrong to dismiss the existing structure as having no merit at all in terms of promoting international cohesion. Baetens Beardsmore and Kohls (op. cit.) found that by the end of the secondary school phase, friendships are cross-national and racism rare, if students stay in the system for a sufficient amount of time. Savvides (2006b, op. cit.) similarly found that although it might seem like several schools running within one large school, European Hours provision helps with integration, although in a later work she also describes some evidence of atomisation, such as the national groupings on school trips (Savvides 2008).

In summary, therefore, we see multiple forms of social sorting taking place within the European schools, and multiple identities co-existing under the same institutional banner. The experiences of children vary greatly according to their ages, nationalities, and prior social backgrounds. Similarly teacher identity can be very different depending on the traditions that have defined the professional practice of individual educators. Much of the academic research in the field indicates that it is length of time within the European Schools System which indicates how close a teacher or student is likely to be to the concept of some sort of 'ideal type' (to use a technical sociological term), aligning well to the traditions and values of the system and thriving within them. However the national and cultural diversity embedded within the European school structures makes defining an ideal type more exact than this somewhat problematic. Nevertheless the next section attempts this, through the lens of citizenship.

Forms of Citizenship

In the absence of what has been described as 'Leitkultur' (Pomerantsev 2016), or in other words, a mainstream model of cultural transmission, citizenship in the European schools cannot rely on simplistic indicators of belonging or nationalism. For example, it would be considered inappropriate within the European schools to pledge allegiance to the EU flag daily, in the manner of American children in relation to the US flag. Similarly the Anthem of Europe is usually absent from everyday schooling, not least because performing it properly would presumably require a full orchestra and four-part choir. There is no single monoculture that prevails. What we do see instead of a cohesive monoculture are various forms of social fragmentation within what is on many levels the same social group (Haas, op. cit.). This is partially due to the elite bilingualism practices amongst students and their parents, as seen in the drive towards non-native speakers joining the English sections of various European schools, as we discussed earlier. Here we see language learning as an active choice, and linked to the concept of what might cautiously be labelled *third culture kids* (Fail 2007), whose identities are international in context as a result of being brought up in a different country during their early years.

There is an additional interplay between citizenship and social class within the educational system here. It is a relatively privileged model where the individual sits at the centre (in this case with personalised timetables and special educational arrangements unique to them alone) with the collective aspects of schooling more peripheral. This has come about purely as a result of the pragmatic arrangements that need to be in place to administer a system as complex as this with any degree of parity and efficiency at all. However a relatively individualistic model such as this also promotes exclusivity, and a by-product may be the development of elites (Swan 1996), as we have seen in the tendency to filter certain types of student out at upper secondary level. This filtering process has its own complexities. The broadly configured European Baccalaureate that students sit at age 18 has been designed around an essentially Francophone model (hence the name) with some aspects of the German *Abitur* system embedded within it, and it is a long way from the British A Level examination, which focuses more on early specialisation and choice. The system is very much an academic one, and does not usefully provide for vocational streams (Marjoram and Williams 1977), although there does seem to have been a single attempt at this. Existing technical and vocational provision is very limited and dates from 1969. It includes: (Group 1) geometric drawing, notions of technology, handicraft; (Group 2) accounting and commercial arithmetic, typewriting, shorthand and commercial correspondence; (Group 3) child care, domestic science and art. These represent short non-academic courses and while still permissible under the regulations, do not seem to be offered any longer in European schools, leaving no vocational programmes at all. Children who don't fit with this elite academic model are regarded as having what Goffman (1963) might describe as a 'spoiled identity' in which they are effectively rejected by the mainstream, leaving to seek an education elsewhere.

We see therefore that citizenship issues are highly complex within the European School System, and yet it is this that is the primary indicator that such schools are needed. Students are in effect a form of temporary migrant, and in transit throughout different EU member states in a way that is difficult to accommodate at a national level (Olsen 2000). Therefore the original founders were correct in understanding that there would be a continuing need for the European schools. However the identity formation of students, and to the same extent teachers, is more often than not a European schools' identity rather than an essentially European one. It would be wrong to make the assumption that just because the curriculum is being taught plurilingually that a European dimension has naturally and automatically developed, despite the best intentions of the founders.

This raises a number of associated issues. Some teachers are concerned there is a concentration on languages yet there is complacency around subject content (for example in the history and geography curricula); they have also expressed concern at the growth of cliques amongst language sections, and whether a Eurocentric identity is possible only at the expense of a truly international one (Savvides 2006b, c). As Savvides argues, it may be that developing a true European identity is elusive, which led to an attempt at a definition in 1988 by the Council of Ministers of Education (Savvides 2008: 8). As Furedi explains, '(i)t is evident that it is far easier to create a European Union than to make people think of themselves or identify as Europeans' (Furedi 2012: 9). This vagueness means that the whole notion of a European identity has suffered from a lack of clarity throughout most of the history of the European schools. It may be that the roots of a European schools' identity lie in a different type of classification and framing. Osler and Starkey talk instead of the idea of 'cosmopolitan citizenship', 'based on feelings of solidarity with fellow human beings wherever they are situated' (Osler and Starkey 2005: 23) and that might be what we are seeing here instead, rather than a European identity in its own right. This brings with it the possibility of international co-operation, but also a potential burden. In the words of one student: '(t)he European School was meant to integrate nationalities but stopped me being integrated into any nation I went to' (Pomerantsev, op. cit.). Whether this is a particular characteristic of the European schools, or a wider problem associated with attending international schools, needs further consideration.

This chapter opened by asking whether the European schools reflected a united and thriving Europe. What is clear is that any answer to this question is a very complex one. The ideology of the European Schools System has its origins in a significantly more limited European project, involving many fewer countries than today, such as Germany, France, Italy, the Netherlands, Belgium and Luxembourg. European expansion to the current 28 member states has led to the European Schools System becoming much more complex and fragmented over time, particularly in the light of key policy changes dating back to the Maastricht Treaty in 1993. This means that while the European Schools System remains separate from the national systems of the countries in which it is hosted, the political tensions currently experienced by Europe are starting to be reflected in its provision.

There are several aspects to this, and in response we see the European Schools System responding on a number of fronts. The pragmatic, plurilingual approach to education it routinely adopts has been challenged by the expansion into Eastern Europe, with many students demanding increased provision of English language teaching, and to a certain degree additional French teaching as well. An increasingly complex web of stakeholders and critics are attempting to renegotiate the basis for provision, and its underlying resource base, particularly in relation to the secondment of teachers from the UK, for example. Admissions policies have come under fire, although to a certain extent this has been ameliorated through the growing provision for accredited schools. This all indicates a system in flux. However within this we see new forms of citizenship emerging. These may indicate a more globalised, international model of integration that reaches beyond the European Schools System itself. In this way, European schools potentially offer a viable alternative to the standard international schooling model frequently based on either the UK or US systems, and a challenge to a monocultural nation state model of education. This sits within a global knowledge economy that has become a reality since 1993 and the Maastricht Treaty.

If the European schools can adapt for the future, ensuring appropriate levels of social inclusion beyond purely the linguistic and citizenship domains, and reflecting the fluid boundaries of modern political life beyond the nation state, there is the potential here for a much more integrated form of European education. This will, however, only happen if it can reach confidently beyond both national and social boundaries, as this form of schooling needs to find a way of appearing relevant to those beyond its immediate circle. In the next chapter we examine the European Baccalaureate and the notion of a final examination.

Open Access This chapter is licensed under the terms of the Creative Commons Attribution 4.0 International License (http://creativecommons.org/licenses/by/4.0/), which permits use, sharing, adaptation, distribution and reproduction in any medium or format, as long as you give appropriate credit to the original author(s) and the source, provide a link to the Creative Commons license and indicate if changes were made.

The images or other third party material in this chapter are included in the chapter's Creative Commons license, unless indicated otherwise in a credit line to the material. If material is not included in the chapter's Creative Commons license and your intended use is not permitted by statutory regulation or exceeds the permitted use, you will need to obtain permission directly from the copyright holder.

5

Schooled and Ready: Assessment Reform

Students in the European School System have since its inception been examined by the European Baccalaureate. The term, Baccalauréat, is used in different ways in different educational systems round the world. In Canada and Belgium it is used to indicate a Bachelor's degree in Francophone universities. In France it refers to the country's national school (lycée) diploma and is equivalent to British 'A' level qualifications. The English Baccalaureate is a performance measure to assess the work of students in secondary schools in England, Wales and Northern Ireland. In Wales, it is also a pre-university qualification. In Spain it refers to a particular form of post-secondary education. The International Baccalaureate Diploma, the oldest and most important of the four International Baccalaureate programmes, is a curriculum for students aged between 16 and 19. In the United States of America a Baccalaureate service is a farewell address given to a graduating class by a teacher or teachers.

The oldest of these is the French Baccalauréat, an academic qualification taken by French students at the end of high school. It thus signals the end of the compulsory period of education in France, typically at the age of eighteen years, and acts as a means of accessing the next stage of education. It was introduced by Napoleon I in 1808. There are other forms of Baccalaureate, such as the International Baccalaureate, but it was originally developed in France. Its most important feature is that it cannot be awarded in a single subject.

Within France, there are three main types of Baccalauréat: the Baccalauréat Général (General Baccalaureate), the Baccalauréat Professionnel (Professional Baccalaureate), and the Baccalauréat Technologique (Technological Baccalaureate). There are some restrictions placed on the type of Baccalaureate that a student can present at some French universities and it doesn't confer automatic rights of entry to any and every French university. Students who are registered for the Baccalauréat Général streams are asked to choose between three streams in their penultimate lycée year. Each of these streams prioritises one specialism over the others; however, this doesn't mean that the student gives up altogether the study of subjects in other streams. Each stream therefore places different weights (coefficients) on each subject.

The Série Scientifique is specifically designed for students who wish to work in scientific fields such as medicine, engineering and the natural sciences. These students are required to specialize in mathematics, physics and chemistry, computer science or earth and life sciences. The Série Économique et Sociale is designed for students who want to eventually pursue careers in the social sciences, management and business administration, and in economics. The most heavily weighted subjects are economics and social sciences and these are only offered in this stream. The Série Littéraire prepares students for careers in the public services. The most important subjects in this stream are philosophy, modern French language and literature, and other modern foreign languages.

If a student is a pupil at a vocational lycée, they can prepare for either the Certificate d'Aptitude Professionelle (CAP) or the Brevet d'Etudes Professionelles (BEP). They can also study for a Brevet des métiers/d'art (BTM or BMA) or a Mention Complementaire (MC). The Brevet d'Etudes Professionelles is considered to be more theoretical than the Certificat d'Aptitude Professionelle, and some students after completing the first of these then go on to study a vocational Baccalaureate such as the Baccalauréat Professionnel. Technological Baccalaureates were introduced in 1968 and are grouped into three Series. The first Series includes engineering, physics, chemistry, biology, medical sciences and microtechnologies. The second Series includes business administration, management, and commercial and computer technologies. The third Series includes the applied arts, computer techniques, and techniques of music and dance. The 1992 Reforms extended this to: industrial science and technology, science and technology laboratory work, tertiary science and technology, medical social sciences and hospitality. As a result of the 2011 reforms, there are now eight Series of technological studies.

The majority of the Baccalauréat examinations take place every June. For lycée students, this is the terminale of the last year. Most of these examinations are of an essay format. The student is given a substantial block of time (depending on the examination, from two to five hours) to complete the written examination, setting out the various arguments around a topic. Mathematics and science examinations involve problem solving, in addition to writing short essays. Students taking foreign language examinations have to be able to translate text as well. In mathematics and the life sciences, the use of questionnaire à choix multiples (multiple choice questions) is in common use. All Baccalaureate students are also required to complete a short research project, known as the travaux personnels encadrés. These are formal examinations, conducted in controlled examination conditions. To further ensure fair marking by the examiners, the test is anonymous, thus eliminating any marking bias that may occur due to favoritism based on sex, religion, national origin or ethnicity.

The principles underpinning the Baccalaureate idea are those of breadth, comprehensiveness, cultural maturation, curriculum integration, allowing weak boundaries between subject disciplines and balancing the demands of specialization with a more rounded and general education. As we have noted, it cannot be awarded in a single subject. Consequently, all the students have to study all the subjects in a curriculum, even if some of these subjects are studied in more depth than others. In theory at least, the Baccalaureate can uniquely provide students with a gestalt (using this term in its original sense) that can act to frame their subsequent life and behaviours. They grow as a person as a result of an individual and cultural maturation or bildung.

The European Baccalaureate

Students in the European schools or in schools accredited by the Board of Governors are examined at the end of their schooling in the system through the European Baccalaureate process, and thus the use of this term refers to a programme of study (two years – S6 and S7 – in this case), an award which has currency in the European Union, and an examination, which is designed to test for knowledge, skills and dispositional elements of the curriculum that the student has followed over the previous two years. As we have seen in Chaps. 2 and 3, the European Baccalaureate cycle consists of a broad multilingual subject-based curriculum, in which students are obliged to take a combination of language, humanities and scientific subjects, with in many cases these subjects being taught through more than one language.

The core curriculum comprises: at least two language subjects (the dominant language and another one); mathematics, either 3 periods/week or 5 periods/week; one scientific subject, either biology 2 periods/week or any other 4-period scientific subject in either biology, chemistry or physics; history and geography, either 2 periods/week or 4 periods/week, which are taught through a different language from the dominant one, either in French, English or German; philosophy, either 2 periods/week or 4 periods/week; physical education; and ethics or religion. In addition to this core curriculum, students choose from a wide range of options, and this amounts to a minimum of 31 periods per week and a maximum of 35 periods each week.

Candidates take three oral examinations (L1, L2 or a subject taught through L2 such as history, geography or economics). Consequently, candidates are required to demonstrate written and oral proficiency in at least two languages. They are also required to take five written examinations: language 1 or advanced language 1, language 2 or advanced language 2, mathematics (5 periods) or mathematics (3 periods), option I (4 periods) and option II (4 periods). The following three factors are taken into consideration for the award of a European Baccalaureate: the average preliminary mark (C) expressed out of 100, the average written examinations mark (W) expressed out of 100, and the average oral examinations mark (O) expressed out of 100. The proportion of the final total mark for the examination allotted to the various parts is as follows: 50% for the average preliminary mark C, 35% for the average W for the written examinations, and 15% for the average O for the oral examinations. The final result is 0.50 C + 0.35 W + 0.15 O.

The preliminary mark is made up of the following: class marks (A marks) and examination marks (B marks). Class marks account for 20 marks out of 50 for the purposes of calculating the preliminary mark (C mark). A class mark is given for each subject taken in year 7 (S7), with the exception of religion/ethics, at the end of each semester. The marks for the examination account for 30 marks out of 50 and are used for the purposes of calculating the preliminary mark (C mark). A mark is given for each subject, with the exception of religion/ethics, on the basis of the results obtained in the examination. Compulsory subjects (with the exception of physical education and religion/ethics), options, and advanced subjects can be the subject of written and oral examinations.

Each examination covers the entire syllabus of the corresponding subject in S7 but is also designed to assess the competences (knowledge, skills and dispositions) acquired in previous years, especially in S6. The marks awarded in both the written and oral examinations are subject to a double moderation and marking by both the candidates' teachers and the external examiners. The final mark is the average of the two examiners' marks. In the case of a mark-disagreement of over two points, a third external moderator is brought in and their task is to establish through a thorough analysis of the previous moderations a final mark between the highest and the lowest awarded by the two previous markers.

Assessment in the European Baccalaureate cycle is criterion-referenced. Though norm-referenced systems of assessment have become less popular, criterion-referenced systems are not without their problems. Systems with a simple pass-fail result such as a driving test are much easier to operate than complex multi-level systems such as the European Baccalaureate. Criteria are relatively easy to identify for use in testing a performance like driving proficiency, but harder to associate precisely with a range of levels of learning as in a school curriculum. In addition, criterion-referenced systems conflate logical hierarchies of skill and content with developmental approaches to the teaching of students. Establishing criteria appropriate to the various levels involves some notion of an average student, which is always difficult to determine. It measures pupils' attainment in relation to the level at which the learning objectives and required competences defined in a given syllabus (in the case we are dealing with here, the European Baccalaureate) have been attained. The European Baccalaureate inspectorate also provides assessment and marking guidelines for criteria for both oral and written examinations.

Assessments may be more or less integrated with the teaching programmes that pupils follow. Some kinds of assessment (for example, IQ tests) are not designed to measure pupil's learning (or the results of a teaching programme), in which case they are often associated with measures of qualities supposedly inherent in the student, such as intelligence. Assessment which is placed at the integrated end of the continuum is likely to be more informal than formal, more formative than summative, process rather than product-orientated, and to be frequent or continuous rather than taking place at one time point, usually at the end of the programme of study. The European Baccalaureate offers greater scope to the designers of the various curricula, because it is better integrated with the programmes of study.

Assessment in the European Baccalaureate is intended to be both formative and summative. Formative assessment focuses on the process of learning. It is reflected in the so called A marks. The A marks represent the pupils' everyday work in a subject, which consists of a variety of tasks and aspects such as: the degree of focus and attention in class; the students' active participation and the quality of their interventions in class; the regularity and consistency of their work in class and at home; how positive their attitude towards the subject is; whether they show signs of initiative, independence and autonomy; and the progress they are making. These forms of formative assessment are in the main attitudinal and can be thought of as regulative devices (i.e. regulating the behavior of the person), rather than learning experiences and assessments of competences.

Summative assessment reflects the performance of a pupil at the end of a given period of instruction. These Baccalaureate examinations are designed to assess the pupils' competences acquired over an extended period of time in a range of subjects. They are held under standardized physical conditions (relating to room arrangements, the use of specific formats, invigilation processes, etc.) and under time constraints. Formative modes of assessment are most closely associated with the process of teaching itself, but it is the results of these summative tests that are most visible and public. Formative dimensions of assessment focus on providing information for the teacher about the way learners complete particular tasks. The information provided is intended to feed directly into the teaching process, so the focus is on how students tackle these tasks and how they go about solving problems that they are given. The assessment environment does not need to be standardized during formative processes of assessment.

Summative assessment is concerned with determining whether students have mastered particular elements of the curriculum. Summative assessments aim to be reliable and valid; and homogeneity of context is considered to be important so that comparability becomes possible. A summative assessment marks some point in the otherwise potentially organic teaching and learning process at which it is decided to stop teaching and give one's full attention to assessment. The stage at which it is most important to carry out this kind of assessment is often determined by factors other than those arising from learning goals, such as predetermined times in the school year, or a requirement to report to other interested parties, as we have seen in the European Baccalaureate.

European Baccalaureate diploma holders enjoy the same rights and benefits as other holders of secondary school-leaving certificates in their countries, including the same right as nationals with equivalent qualifications to seek admission to any university or institution of tertiary education in the European Union. This issue is an important one and we discuss it in more detail in Chap. 6.

In 2007 the Board of Governors commissioned an external evaluation of the European Baccalaureate, the objectives of which were: to determine its fitness for purpose, its quality, the extent of its recognition by the member states, and whether it was in a fit state to be offered to students outside the European schools. The Report was received in 2008 and, though this is to some extent the fault of the specification of work given to the evaluators, it failed to adequately address the make-up, both in a practical and normative sense, of the internal and external relations of the Baccalaureate, focusing on a small number of technical issues, at the expense of examining fundamental curriculum and assessment principles.

The evaluators, Cambridge Assessment, argued that there were no curriculum incoherencies or grossly inappropriate contents, approaches, or demands in the European Baccalaureate. They did however, identify one subject, Geography, which appeared to require urgent review. It is worth reminding ourselves that this review was completed in 2008, and that a lot has changed since then in the programmes of study. They further argued that there was a relatively restricted range of subjects, suggesting the possibility of including business-related and applied subjects, non-European languages, drama and media studies in the curriculum. Science syllabuses, they suggested, should be updated and a stronger and more coherent approach to the development of enquiry-based and investigative skills established.

The European Baccalaureate involves a high volume of internal assessment by teachers. This, they argued, is a potential strength, establishes an integrated learning and assessment model and makes a positive contribution to its validity. However, while European Baccalaureate teachers are very experienced, opportunities for ensuring that all teachers have access to early induction and standards training, they suggested, were vital. The extent to which common standards can be shown to apply across all subjects was also an issue for the evaluators in the marking of the final examinations where systems of marking review across subjects, between examiners and across years are not well-defined.

Greater clarity would be achieved, they suggested, by statements of actual time in the programme. In terms of weightings between different parts of the programme, the evaluators were of the view that the value contributed by the internal assessment of preliminary marks should be retained. Proposals for a revised weighting of written examinations relative to L1 and L2 oral examinations, they argued, would seem to overstate the contribution which a student's oral performance in languages made to their overall European Baccalaureate score, particularly for those students who were preparing for science, medicine and engineering courses at university. The practice of double marking, they suggested, should be reviewed, and the evaluators urged the European Baccalaureate curriculum developers to move towards 'virtual' standardization approaches, particularly using digitised scripts and on-line marking.

Significantly, they argued in their Report, all examinations should be regarded as 'high stakes'. Those examinations, which mark the end of secondary education and provide for progression to university, are of the highest importance to individuals and impose rigorous standards of accountability on assessment bodies. Finally, the evaluators considered that the adoption of quality models such as ISO 9001 certification or the quality assurance procedures developed by the Association of Language Testers in Europe (ALTE) would be of value. They urged the European Baccalaureate to also consider the establishment of its own Code of Practice to complement the more administratively oriented focus of the arrangements for implementing it. Some of these suggestions have been taken up by the European Baccalaureate curriculum makers, though none of them address the fundamental tensions and difficulties caused by the conflation of formative and summative purposes, the poor use of coursework processes, the confusions surrounding oral assessments (their use should be commensurate with their capacity to validly assess some aspect of the curriculum), and the inclusion of regulative activities in assessment processes (as they are currently expressed in the assessment arrangements).

Reorganising the European Baccalaureate

In 2015 we wrote a report about the European Baccalaureate, in the form of an evaluation of a proposal for the reorganisation of secondary studies in the European Schools for secondary years 4, 5, 6 and 7 (cf. Leaton-Gray et al. 2015). The objectives of the study were to establish and demonstrate the impact of the proposed new structure for secondary studies (i.e. levels S4–S7, though reference is also made to S1–S3 on the grounds that forms of progression and curriculum coherence require consideration of lower secondary as well as upper secondary studies), compared to the current situation. And in addition we sought to determine whether and to what extent the proposals: met the principles stated in the Convention; ensured access to European secondary and tertiary education systems; took into account the mandate given by the Board of Governors; took into account the needs of pupils faced with the demands of the modern world; were relevant, coherent, comprehensive, and allowed breadth of study for all pupils in the system; conformed to the accepted and logical principles of curriculum design; and guaranteed in the last two years, leading to the European Baccalaureate, a general education around the eight key competences for lifelong learning.

Our suggestions were comprehensive and in accord with the principles that underpin the construction of productive learning environments. We suggested that Baccalaureate rules should be amended so that each student takes eight examinations; the determination of each of these examinations, i.e. whether they should include oral, coursework and/or written papers, and the relations between them, is discussed below. We argued that forms of discriminatory groupings, such as streaming, setting, multi-age and multi-grade arrangements, should be minimised insofar as resources within the system and institutions allow this to happen. The nine-year upper tenure limit for European schools' teachers, and the loss of organizational knowledge that is associated with removing these skilled practitioners at the end of their tenure, often to be replaced with a Chargé de Cours (locally hired) teacher who is not appointed via the same route, was one of our strongest recommendations. This was to ensure that the European Schools Systems and its various institutions, i.e. the schools, retained their institutional memories. In addition, candidates, we suggested, should take eight examinations: language and communication (L1), mathematics, language and communication (L2), humanities, expressive and performative studies, science, social studies, option 1 and option 2. In both option slots, students should choose between streams. They should only be allowed to make one choice from their stream in this pathway.

Each examination should consist of four elements: coursework, practical, oral and a written paper. The proportion of the final total mark for the examination allotted to the various parts as a result should depend on the curriculum content (i.e. knowledge constructs, skills and dispositions) of the subject area. In other words, not every subject should be tested through all four elements, but only through those elements that refer to the type of curriculum content of the subject. For example, language and communication (L1) should be tested through 30% coursework (C), 20% oral (O) and 50% written examination (WE). The final result would then be $0.30 \, C + 0.20 \, O + 0.50 \, WE$. Class marks should no longer be awarded as this is a summative examination. Orals and practicals should be conducted one month before the date of the examination in each subject. Coursework, oral and practical completion and assessment rules would need to be written, with the following principles applied. Each task is criterion-referenced with those criteria being open and available to students. Marks are allocated to each criterion and made public. The work should be completed in non-regulated settings. It should be marked by the teacher, sample-moderated by the Baccalaureate office, and sample-moderated by an external examiner (to the system), who in addition benchmarks the marking against comparable systems. Marks would not be released until the final examination result had been declared. These are practical recommendations. However, they should only be developed with regards to a full understanding of assessment and examination practices.

Examinations

Here we focus on the general notion of assessment in its many guises and forms. All of these manifestations reflect decisions that have been made and will be made in the future about who and what is assessed, for what reason and in what way, and they all reflect a particular social context. What this means is that the particular forms of assessment that are adopted are dependent on how those social contexts are and have been constructed. The underlying principle when we are dealing with assessment practices is that educational assessment must be understood as a social practice. Moreover, although it is possible to trace policy issues in assessment back to the earliest days of public examinations when, for example, the Emperor Napoleon recognized the powerful contribution nationally controlled assessment procedures could play in cementing national unity, in recent years the importance of assessment as a policy tool has grown enormously as governments and education systems have increasingly come to realize its powerful potential as a mechanism of social control.

For Michael Foucault (1979), the examination combines the techniques of an observing hierarchy and those of a normalizing judgment.

The examination therefore enables society to construct individuals in particular ways. Knowledge of persons is created which has the effect of binding individuals to each other, embedding those individuals in networks of power and sustaining mechanisms of surveillance, which are all the more powerful because they work by allowing individuals to govern themselves. The examination introduced a whole new mechanism that in effect both contributed to a new type of knowledge formation and constructed a new network of power, all the more persuasive once it had become established throughout society.

This mechanism works in three ways: firstly, by transforming what can be seen and observed into an exercise of power; secondly, by introducing the idea of the individual into the field of documentation; and thirdly, by turning each individual into a case. In the first instance, disciplinary power is exercised invisibly and this contrasts with the way power networks in the past operated visibly, through the explicit exercise of force. This invisibility works by imposing on subjects a notion of objectivity that acts to bind them to a truth about that examination, a truth that people find hard to resist. The examined person understands themself in terms of criteria that underpin that process, not least that they are successful or unsuccessful. The examination therefore works by arranging objects or people in society.

In the second instance, the examination allows the individual to be archived by being inscribed textually. An attempt is made to position these knowledge-development activities as contributing to better and more progressive framings of society. Over the last twenty years in schools in Europe, the proliferation and extension of assessment through such devices as key stage tests, records of achievement, examined course work, education certificates, and school reports, and evaluation through such devices as school inspection, teacher appraisal, profiles and the like, means that teachers and students are increasingly subject to disciplinary regimes of individual measurement and assessment which have the further effect of determining them as cases.

The third of Foucault's modalities refers to the objectification of the individual as a branch of knowledge, so that the individual can now be described, judged, measured and compared with others. One final point needs to be made about the examination, and this is that for the first time the individual could be scientifically and objectively categorized and characterized through a modality of power where difference becomes the most relevant factor. Hierarchical normalization becomes the dominant way of organizing society. Foucault is suggesting here that the examination itself, seemingly a neutral device, in reality acts to position the person being examined in a discourse of normality, so that for them to understand themselves in any other way is to understand themselves as abnormal and even as unnatural. This positioning works to close off the possibility of the persons being examined of seeing themselves in any other way, though it may not be successful.

Assessment serves a wide range of purposes, ranging from the most commonplace of exchanges in a restaurant for example to school reports and high-stakes examinations, from individual job interviews to national monitoring. What unites all of these is the sense in which assessment first and foremost is a proxy for determining the quality of something or someone. It therefore operates as a mechanism for placing that person or object in a particular hierarchy of values: this person is better than this other person with regards to a particular range of skills and this school is better than this other school because its students have graduated with better examination results. This spectrum of communication ranges from the most informal of exchanges to the extremely formal, spanning everything from school reports to high-stakes public examinations, and from individual job interviews to national monitoring, the common factor being the use of assessment data of one kind or another as a publicly acceptable code for quality. Closely associated with this is the issue of legitimacy. The results of any particular assessment device have to be trusted by the public if the consequences are to be acceptable. Sadly, assessment issues are generally treated as technical matters, as focusing on improving the methodologies used to assess people rather than on the purposes or consequences of using such approaches. We can see this most clearly in the 2008 Evaluation of the European Baccalaureate by Cambridge Associates.

What this in effect means is that on occasions clear contradictions and tensions between common assessment practices emerge. An example of this is the incompatibility between policies and practices, which lead to an increasingly test-driven educational and curricular culture as well as an explicit commitment to lifelong learning processes. Another example might be the tension between summative and formative purposes in an assessment. This learning agenda, exemplified in the notion of formative assessment, is at odds with the use of punitive high-stakes testing, which has as its principle purpose raising standards, though the notion of a standard is in itself a contentious issue. Another tension within the system focuses on the more or less contradictory pressures of maintaining and indeed even increasing enrolment whilst at the same time keeping standards high and ensuring that the public have confidence in those standards. Dore's (1976) now classic study of qualification inflation showed how the interaction between the supply of qualifications and the availability of employment opportunities tended to result in the pursuit of ever-higher levels of qualification as a form of educational inflation.

Internationalization of Assessment

An extremely important aspect of assessment is its increasing internationalization, exemplified by large-scale cross-national assessment studies, such as the Programme for International Student Assessment (PISA). Andreas Schleicher (2013), from the Organization for Economic Cooperation and Development (OECD), uses a methodology that involves the ranking of a variety of countries in relation to their performance on a series of tests, and then the identification of those systemic elements that are present in high performing countries and not present in low-performing countries. From this he concludes that it is possible to identify the optimum conditions for a system's effectiveness. He is therefore able to suggest that: children from similar social backgrounds can show very different performance levels, depending on the school they go to or the country they live in; there is no relationship between the share of students with an immigrant background in a country and the overall performance of students in that country; there is no relation between class size and learning outcomes within or across countries (the conceptual framework he works to here makes the unjustified assumption that all the different types of learning activities are optimally performed with the same class size); there is no incompatibility between the quality of learning and equity since the highest performing education systems combine both; all students are capable of achieving high standards; and more generally, top performing education systems tend to be more rigorous, with fewer curriculum items and with these being taught in greater depth.

The approach has a number of flaws in its conceptualisation and application. The first of these is that an assumption is made that a person has a knowledge, skill or dispositional set, which is configured in a particular way (i.e. it has a grammar), and it is this knowledge, skill or dispositional set, or at least elements of it, which is directly assessed when that person is tested. In contrast, any testing that is carried out with the purpose of determining whether these attributes are held, not held, or even partially held by an individual, always involves an indirect process of examination, where the additional element is a conjecture, retroduction, inference or best guess.

A second false belief is that this grammar is organised into elements, there are relations between those elements, and each element can be scaled, which can then be directly investigated. This can be contrasted with a position which suggests that, in the application of the knowledge, skill or dispositional set, whether for the purposes of testing or for use in everyday life, a range of other knowledge elements, skills and dispositions are referred to. There is, therefore, a set of factors that in combination may result in construct-irrelevance variance (cf. Messick 1989), that is, variance amongst a population of testees as a result of factors that do not have anything to do with the construct being tested. Even if knowledge of or competence in the construct is equally distributed in this population, some testees will do better than others (that is, on their actual scores) and this is not because they have greater knowledge or are more competent in the construct being tested. This might involve either construct-under-representation or construct-over-representation, and within the confines of the test itself it is impossible to determine which of these has occurred.

A third false belief is that in the use of a knowledge-set, or in the performance of a skill, or in the application of a disposition, no internal transformation takes place. There is also an external transformative process at work, and thus a fourth false belief is that testing a person's knowledge, skills and aptitudes has no washback effects on either the original knowledge construct, or the internally transformed knowledge set ready for testing. In contrast, the well-documented process of washback works in just this way, so that instead of the assessment acting merely as a descriptive device, it also acts in a variety of ways to transform the construct it is seeking to measure.

A fifth false belief is that the process of testing works in a unidirectional linear fashion. For example, a person knows something, that person is subjected to a test which is designed to test for traces of that learning in a population of knowers with similar characteristics, and a score in relation to that construct is recorded indicating that the person either knows it, doesn't know it or knows it to some extent. No consideration is given to bidirectionality, incorporating forward and backward flows, so that the taking of the test and the recording of the mark impact on and influence the original knowledge construct. This changes the structure (both quantitatively and qualitatively) of the construct, and its affordances, making the original determination of it and them unreliable.

A sixth false belief is that different types of knowledge, including those at different levels of abstraction, can be tested using the same algorithmic process; and a seventh false belief is that the performance on the test represents to a greater or lesser extent (given that the person may have been distracted or constrained in some way or another) what the testee can do or show, rather than there being a qualitative difference between the performance on the test and the construct, skill, or disposition of the testee. An individual may have to reframe their knowledge set to fit the test, and therefore the assessment of their mastery of the construct is not a determination of their capacity in relation to the original construct, but a determination of whether they have successfully understood how to rework their capacity to fit the demands of the testing technology.

An eighth false belief is that a test can be constructed which is culture-free or free of those issues that disadvantage some types of learners at the expense of others. The extent of cultural bias in the PISA tests is unrealised and certainly under-reported. In addition, a particular technical problem with PISA relates to its sampling procedures. If different types of sampling in the different countries are used, then some of these countries will be disadvantaged compared with others. Sampling issues are present in any test, whether they refer to selecting children from a number of grade levels and not specifying proportions from each grade, to selecting parts of countries for reporting purposes and ignoring the rest, as in the 2015 PISA tests (OECD 2016), where only the richest and better educated cohort of learners was entered (from Shanghai), and these were allowed to represent China as a whole, to the selective (by the individual country) non-participation of some types of schools in some countries and not others. Cultural differences take a number of different forms, such as, ascribing different values, and different strengths of values to cultural items, or determining the nature, quality, probative force, relevance-value and extent of evidence, or focusing on practices which may be more familiar to people in some countries and less so in others. However, more importantly, cultural differences with regards to the selection of test items refer to the expression of the problem to be solved. If, for example, different national idioms, different national ways of thinking embedded in language forms, and different normic values woven into the fabric of national discourses are ignored, then the presentation of the actual test items as well as the range of possible answers that can be given may favour students from one nation at the expense of students from another.

There are a number of ways of identifying good practice within a system of education. The first is identifying outputs from the system (these can be test scores, dispositional elements, acquired skills, ethical and moral qualities); that is, outputs that have resulted from the individual's participation in the system itself. The argument is then made that one system is better than another because it has better outputs, and, further to this, that the characteristics of these national systems should be bottled up and transferred to those countries or jurisdictions or systems which are considered not to be successful or effective in these terms. It is interesting that the European School system is wedded to the use of quantifying, reductionist and in some cases misleading measures to determine whether it is successful or not.

If the information collected about individuals in a system of education at the end of their time spent in the system is used to make judgements about the quality of provision within them, then there are two possibilities: raw scores – student scores are aggregated to allow comparative judgements to be made about these schools, districts, states or nation states; and value-added scores – value-added data analysis models the input of particular institutions or systems, such as schools, in relation to the development of individuals that belong to those institutions or systems. As a result of these processes, a value can be attached to the input of the educational institution or nation as it has impacted on the progress of the individual(s) who attended it, or been a part of it. The accuracy of such modelling depends on the belief that the educational researcher has in the reliability and validity of the data that is used, in the decisions they make about which variables to use in the modelling process, and also in the ability of the researcher to develop appropriate indicators or quasi-properties to reflect the actual properties of individuals, educational institutions and nations, and their covariance in real-life settings. This in theory allows one to make comparative judgements between students, schools, districts, states or nation states, though all the systems that have been devised and used have in one way or another proved to be unsatisfactory.

A further way of determining quality in a system is by identifying a norm so as to allow a comparison to be made. For example, a system of education, whether international, national or local (or even cross-national as in the European School System) can be compared with, and marked against, a model of best practice, where this model is constructed in terms of the inclusion of all the possible elements that could and should form an education system (i.e. structures, institutions, curricula, pedagogic arrangements and evaluative procedures), their arrangement in the most logical way (for example, that curricular intentions should precede pedagogical approaches and indeed derive their credibility from these curricular intentions), and the identification and enactment of logically formed relational arrangements between these elements (i.e. that evaluative washback mechanisms should not be allowed to distort the curriculum as it was originally conceived). The norm that is used comparatively is constructed through sound logical and philosophical foundational principles. And in addition the meaning of concepts is treated as an empirical matter, as to how they are used in communities. A reliance on outputs in the comparative process is unsafe and more importantly likely to be invalid. The preferred methodological approach then becomes a searching for mechanisms, relations and structures that are potentially causally efficacious, can be contextualised (historically, culturally and socio-economical), but can also contribute to human wellbeing. And in turn this would involve the avoidance of reductionist and decontextualized accounts (such as in Mourshed et al. 2010) of how education systems round the world operate.

What it is possible to argue is that there is now a world trade in educational policies, especially in relation to assessment issues. This policy borrowing, the take-up of apparently good ideas developed in one country by another, has further strengthened the grip of conventional assessment assumptions. Despite the significant evidence concerning flaws in international comparisons of student achievement, the power of the simple messages that can be and are derived from them about relative national success in a world of increasingly global competition has acted to reinforce the prevailing domination of established forms of educational assessment.

Validity and Use

Samuel Messick (1989), some time ago, argued that the validity of assessment practices inheres in the consequences that follow from their use. The impact of assessment on the lives of individuals is becoming more widespread and serious with its growing importance across the world. It follows that there is clearly a need for more thorough explorations of both the validity and the reliability of the various approaches to designing and interpreting the test data that are commonly used by governments (and by education systems such as the European School system) and which command the confidence of a public which does not understand the technical limitations. The research data show that current policies are ill-informed, and are almost certainly far from the best, though rich and varied.

Some of the defining aspects of recent assessment research stand out with quite remarkable clarity. Chief amongst these is the increase in assessment activity of all kinds and the penetration of assessment in its various guises into almost every aspect of human endeavour. We have become assessment societies, as wedded to our belief in the power of numbers, grades, targets and league tables to deliver quality and accountability, equality and defensibility as we are to modernism itself. History will readily describe the 1990s and 2000s as 'the assessment era', when belief in the power of assessment to provide a rational, efficient and publicly acceptable mechanism of judgement and control reached its high point across the world.

The assessment revolution has been one of scale, range and significance; a revolution that has elevated quantitative data, the raw material of most public assessment, as the principal mechanism for delivering transparency, accountability and predictability. The collection of data has become in itself a major instrument of social control, whether this is at the level of the individual, the institution or indeed whole operational systems such as that of education.

All these various criticisms are helping to challenge the assumptions on which most of the existing edifices of assessment have been built. Belief in the power of conventional summative assessment techniques to be objective and efficient, to motivate present performance and to predict future performance, is being challenged by a range of research evidence that identifies significant flaws in these assumptions. Moreover, the assumptions highlight the worrying consequences that the use of assessment to measure and control has, including reduced motivation and significantly lower performance on the part of students.

Much of the familiar contemporary apparatus of assessment technologies was born of the modernist assumptions and educational needs of the nineteenth century. The assumptions informing these approaches can be identified as: the capacity to seek to identify relative levels of student performance as the basis for educational selection; to undertake such identification with a sufficient degree of objectivity that it provides a broadly fair outcome for the candidates affected; that the quality of such assessment is embodied in notions of reliability and validity; that students' scores on national examinations and tests provide a valid indicator of the quality of institutional performance; and that it is possible usefully to compare the productivity of individual education systems through international comparisons.

Assessment standards can be used in a number of different ways, with different consequences. They can be used to determine whether and in what way the individual is meeting them, as well as providing information about how the individual can perform better in the future. Learning and assessment practices on the learning programme can be regarded as formative if: there is evidence of the student's achievement; that evidence is elicited, interpreted, and used by the teacher, the individual student and their fellow students; and such evidence is used by the teacher with the specific intention of deciding on the subsequent steps in the teaching-and-learning process (i.e. 'instruction' with the intention of further developing learning). The interaction between the teacher and their student(s) is formative when it influences the learner's cognition: the teacher's external stimulus and feedback triggers an internal production by the individual student. Or they can be used to summarise levels of achievement at group, school or national levels. In summary, they can be used summatively or formatively. In the European School System, summative forms of assessment take priority over formative forms of assessment, sometimes to the detriment of learning processes.

In the next chapter we examine the external relations of the system; that is, the relations between the European schools and the EU higher education system; relations between the curriculum offered in the European schools and the curriculum and assessment arrangements in European nations; and the relations between the European Baccalaureate and other Baccalaureate and final examinations systems in the rest of Europe.

Open Access This chapter is licensed under the terms of the Creative Commons Attribution 4.0 International License (http://creativecommons.org/licenses/by/4.0/), which permits use, sharing, adaptation, distribution and reproduction in any medium or format, as long as you give appropriate credit to the original author(s) and the source, provide a link to the Creative Commons license and indicate if changes were made.

The images or other third party material in this chapter are included in the chapter's Creative Commons license, unless indicated otherwise in a credit line to the material. If material is not included in the chapter's Creative Commons license and your intended use is not permitted by statutory regulation or exceeds the permitted use, you will need to obtain permission directly from the copyright holder.

6

Consolidating the Work of Their Fathers: Moving on from European Schools to Higher Education

Equal right of access to national Higher Education systems is enshrined in EU law for holders of the European Baccalaureate, or school-leavers' certificate. Although many students are able to access even the most elite of universities and the most competitive of courses, the path to higher education does not always run smoothly. Consequently some parents and students sometimes describe feeling as though they are caught in a certain degree of educational and political crossfire. Others feel the European Schools approach is not suitable, and leave the system as a consequence. In the light of these concerns, the chapter discusses the relationship of the European Baccalaureate to national and international university entrance processes. It gives examples from our recent research into how the European schools' curriculum, and its related assessment processes, map across to a number of university courses. It also relates this to aspects of the lived experience of university through the eyes of alumni, their parents, and their tutors, drawing on our own research findings.

When considering the relationship of the EU schools to higher education, it is necessary to take into account four different categories of external relations. These are: the European schools' own admissions policies, repeaters and leavers associated with the European Schools System, higher education admissions, and the relationship with national schools systems. We now examine each in turn.

Admissions

As we discussed in Chap. 4, the admissions rules for European schools are relatively complex and have recently become even more so as the system has developed over time. Earlier we identified two types of school: Category I and Category II (Accredited) schools. In the former type, admissions priority is given to certain categories of employee directly employed by the European Commission, making the European schools a kind of 'company school' for practical purposes. The unintended consequence of this policy is that priority is given to certain nationalities, in particular the Germans (12.6% of the overall total of students), the French (12.1%), the Italians (9.9%), the Belgians (10.3%) and the Spanish (8.5%). (Data from Board of Governors of European schools.)

This has also meant a distinct lack of access to the children of those in supporting roles who are also part of the Brussels machinery, such as outsourced ancillary workers, journalists and lobbyists. While notionally they can also apply for places in the European Schools, they must pay to attend, unlike those directly employed by the Commission, and in addition there may not be sufficient space for these students, as they are in the lowest category of priority. Therefore we see a core group of bureaucrats who are able to benefit most extensively from the provision on offer, with others occupying a more peripheral position, causing some resentment amongst the local population and leading to problems of legitimacy (Van Parijs 2009). This represents a distinctive grouping in which there is a form of social reproduction taking place, with highly qualified, graduate professionals schooling their children together in a system that suits their particular professional needs. However this is less so potentially in Category II (Accredited) schools, as these are open to all; however, as they are fee-paying this means selection on ability to pay, once again is going to make access easier for children of graduate or professional parents. It is also likely that they will represent more closely the nationalities of the countries in which they are located. Overall this is a system very much geared up to a student body that is expected to access higher education in the future (as opposed to predominantly vocational training, or unskilled work).

Repeaters and Leavers

It is important to understand that there are different categories of leaver, and this is because leaving can mean one of three things. It could be a transfer *between* European schools due to parental career changes within the Commission or other European institutions, a transfer *out* of the European Schools System back into the national system of origin, once again because of parental careers, or it could mean leaving the system because of perceived student/school/system incompatibility.

In the former cases, this is a reasonable step given that the unproblematic flow in, out and across European Schools is the primary purpose for their existence. This is not therefore likely to disrupt university admissions to any significant extent. However in the latter case, where a student has left because he or she experienced difficulties with the particular educational model adopted by the European schools, this is more likely to have a particular impact on access to higher education in the medium to long term, either for academic or psychological reasons. In academic terms, there might have been disruption to a student's studies for some reason, and in psychological terms this may have led to a degree of *anomie* or alienation as we discussed in Chap. 4. This runs the risk of acting as a form of progression 'road block' in terms of a student's education in later years.

How likely this is depends on where and when a student encounters the European Schools System. It is well known that repeat rates vary across different European Schools, and the latest available data show that the range is from 0.3% (Frankfurt) to 2.0% (Bergen). Additionally, we found that repeat rates vary across school years, with a large increase occurring in S4 and S5. At this time, a student repeating a school year was also more likely to leave the European Schools System altogether. Therefore some educational routes through the system present more hazards to students than others in terms of likelihood of academic failure, and with it the likelihood of longer-term problems, particularly with regards to higher education progression.

The European Schools and Higher Education Admissions

As part of the movement towards closer union, there were attempts to make European university admissions simpler, and this was one important focus of the Lisbon Treaty of 2004. It is also evidenced in the Bologna process from 2005 onwards. During Bologna there were attempts at standardising entry across Europe as well as qualification systems and structures, as a means of co-operation, particularly with regard to the qualifications framework for the European Higher Education Area (EHEA). Mobility was strongly encouraged via EHEA, and it specified the attributes that students could expect after participating in various cycles of education. This was also supported by the Erasmus scheme, which encouraged youth mobility.

Regardless of nationality, a large number (50% plus) of European schools' students routinely take advantage of the mobility opportunities open to them, and apply to universities in the UK via the UCAS (Universities and Colleges Admissions Service) system. This is regardless of any considerations surrounding university fees. Any concerns are likely to be offset by the ability of EU students to apply for student loans on the same basis as UK ones, although whether this will change in the future is unclear. It may be that the Bologna 'scorecards' are a factor here, with UK universities being recognised as being high quality in terms of overall degree structure, quality assurance processes and degree recognition internationally (European Commission 2011). Within the UK, many of these students attend Russell Group (top international research) universities, including the elite universities of Oxford and Cambridge. The remaining half is distributed across Europe, the United States, and Canada, with some students attending university in Australia and New Zealand. Destination data is not collected in any systematic sense centrally by careers advisors or the Office of the Secretary General. However during our 2014–2015 study we were able to gain access to application patterns in one elite university, Cambridge.

In the academic year 2013–2014, Cambridge University received 98 applications from 14 schools offering the European Baccalaureate (the

University only makes a distinction on the basis of qualification rather than whether a candidate has attended a Category 1 or Category 2 European School, for example.) Candidates applied to 22 of the standard age colleges, and to 18 of Cambridge's 25 undergraduate courses. Given the number of applicants this was considered by the University to be a good spread; the only feature of note is that one third applied to study Natural Sciences and Engineering. Cambridge admitted 16 of those students, or 16.3%. Though this is lower than the overall success rate for students applying to the University (c. 22%), it is reported as being higher than the success rate for students not at UK schools (c. 13%). Successful applicants are typically asked for 85–90% overall, with 90% in subjects most closely related to the course they wish to study. This would suggest that candidates from European schools during the academic year 2013–2014 were being accepted at roughly the rate that might be expected, given the spread of nationalities and backgrounds, and that the percentage being requested was reasonable in terms of discriminating amongst students to find those most suited to an elite university education (roughly equivalent to A*AA and A*A*A for the Natural Sciences in terms of UK Advanced Level examinations). We felt in the light of this that there may be merit in continuing to track admissions with reference to how long individual students had spent in (a) the British education system, (b) the European Schools System, and (c) other systems within Europe and internationally, to ascertain whether there is any relationship between the length of time in any particular system, transfers in or out of systems at particular times, and successful applications to elite universities in the UK.

In addition to the Cambridge University applications data, we had access to a limited dataset from Culham School, which is based in the UK. When we spoke to different stakeholders as we were gathering data during our study, anecdotal accounts suggested that some parents perceived problems when students are applying to highly competitive university courses. We could not find much hard evidence to support or refute this given the limited resources available to us. During the period 2009–2013, 256 students from this school went on to further and higher education. 83% of these students enrolled in UK institutions, and of this group, 62% achieved places at Russell Group universities including Oxford and Cambridge. This represents roughly three times as many successful Russell Group applicants as would be normally expected from the general applicant population. Outside the UK, 8 Culham students were accepted by the elite Sciences-Po in France during this period, and two at MIT and Berkeley in the USA. From this it seemed that the elite/research university pattern of successful applications was broadly similar to that of many selective independent schools in the UK, and therefore when compared to the Cambridge University data, the position of EU Schools students looked significantly more secure than perhaps some parents considered it to be.

As a result of the internationally diverse application patterns of students, within the European Schools system there is a similarly broad understanding of different entry requirements in different countries and institutions, as you would expect. However amongst the stakeholders we spoke to, there was also criticism of the European Baccalaureate not being fully understood. In addition, we came across some isolated misunderstandings about particular British entry requirements and expectations (for example it was categorically stated to us by one member of a committee that a particular combination of Chemistry and Art was needed for Architecture degree courses, and a combination of History and Chemistry was needed for Archaeology degree courses, as a justification for particular minority subject combinations being made possible within the Baccalaureate. These are not conventional combinations within the British system by any means, and when we checked, they were not specified by any universities as a UCAS entry requirement, so we can only assume from this that a combination of parental anxieties and pressures had led to the assumption).

Another reason to suppose that university admissions practices are reasonably consistent is that in the UK, explicit guidance has been given to university admissions officers in order to ensure a full understanding of the European Baccalaureate qualification (Department for Education 2013). Within this document, the qualification is described as 'demanding' and it is made clear that candidates are expected to perform well across a range of subjects. It should be noted that, as part of the UK university entry process, candidates are required to complete a centralised Universities and Colleges Admissions Service application form, known as the 'UCAS' form. It is made clear in the Department for Education (DfE) guidance document that on this form, candidates may give their S6 results, with some additional S5 results if this is felt to be appropriate. The document states clearly that around half of European School applicants to UK universities are likely to be non-British or Irish nationals and many will therefore not have studied English as their mother tongue, but that further proof of proficiency in English should not be required. Typical offers to candidates have included specifying an overall European Baccalaureate score (as a percentage), or specifying an overall European Baccalaureate score (%) combined with marks out of 10 in specific subjects. In addition to this, institutions are given specific guidance on making offers with respect to four points:

- Offers asking only for a final EB score are seen as most suitable for subjects requiring a broad education, with evidence of attainment across a wide curriculum.
- For degree courses not requiring any specific subject knowledge on entry, the DfE advises that breadth of the EB should be seen as an advantage.
- For courses prescribing certain A level subjects, institutions may wish to specify the marks to be attained in particular subjects.
- It would be very unusual to specify marks in more than three subjects, even for the most competitive courses. (Department for Education 2013: 16)

This document has been widely circulated amongst UK university admissions officers and from our informal enquiries, there appears to be good recognition of the qualification overall. In other non-English speaking countries there is often less selection for university entrance, and this would mean in many cases that for all but the most competitive courses, such as Medicine, European Schools graduates holding the Baccalaureate would be automatically eligible for university places.

Other European National and Independent School Systems

As we have discussed throughout this book, the European Schools System is designed to align to each of the national systems, and this is supported through the engagement of Government-sponsored teachers from each member state, as well as the engagement of school inspectors from each member state. Its aim is to allow free movement of students at different stages of their academic careers and this includes university, which is why a clear relationship between the European Baccalaureate and university entrance has been enshrined in law. As it states in Article 5 (2), holders of the Baccalaureate should:

1. Enjoy, in the member state of which they are nationals, all the benefits attaching to the possession of the diploma or certificate awarded at the end of secondary school education in that country; and
2. Be entitled to seek admission to any university in the territory of any member state on the same terms as nationals of that member state with equivalent qualifications

The system is designed to be a comprehensive schooling system, with all students having the opportunity of sitting the final examination. However as we have argued previously, the student body is closer to those who attend a French Lycee or a German Gymnasium, or selective independent or grammar schools in the UK, making it more representative of families with graduate or professional parents. Therefore, the European Schools System is potentially aligned more to some types of school than others, and very close to the upper end of the highly stratified UK educational system, described by Hansen and Vignoles in some depth (Hansen and Vignoles 2005).

In terms of this social alignment, there are a number of striations, which it is useful to consider. Here we mean striations in the Deleuzian sense (cf. Deleuze 1968) of a flow along particular paths, rather than a smooth, equal distribution. With regards to the European schools, six primary striations are considered: intelligence, social class, gender, race, sexuality and dis(ability).

Social Striations

The existence of international elite bilinguals within the system indicates a form of higher social status, as we suggested in Chap. 4. A combination of language skills, as well as being embedded within a multinational and multicultural system, means that students develop supra-national identities that reflect the globalised graduate status of their parents. Another indicator of this particular homogenisation of social class is the fact that the original vocational programme, formerly developed in the 1960s, has been allowed to degrade over time and is no longer offered. This is because for the dominant social group it has no particular relevance. University entrance has become the goal.

To put this into a wider context, students are entering a system in which an individual's ability to enter university is extensively linked to parental education and income levels, something that is also a characteristic of the UK education system (Hansen and Vignoles 2005) and which goes a long way to explaining the large number of applications to UK universities. Stratified higher education systems such as this are likely to be the places most attractive and familiar to the average European schools' graduate. In a high-skills, knowledge-intensive, economy, this makes sense at a personal level, but overall the system ignores other social groups in its quest for international mobility for its students. As Van Parijs (2009) writes,

> It is not good for the offspring of the EU's bureaucracy to grow up in such a socially homogeneous environment. Nor is it good for a city like Brussels to have part of its school population creamed off by what amounts to an invidious apartheid regime: when you are admitted to an elite school by virtue of the status of your parents, it is hard not to develop a feeling of superiority towards those who are not.

Given that the European Schools are co-educational, divisions surrounding gender within this schooling system are less significant than they might otherwise be. This can largely be attributed to a clear resistance to early specialisation. Maintaining student involvement with all categories of academic subjects, ranging from the humanities to the sciences and mathematics, means that some of the gendered subject engagement patterns that exist in other countries are less of an issue here. By contrast, the original vocational programme from the 1960s was highly gendered, but as we have said, it no longer exists.

There is provision for Specific Learning Difficulties and to some extent physical disabilities, as well as a dedicated school inspector for this area of operation, but the competitive nature of the academic environment can mean that certain students are eased out of the system over time, or do not apply in the first instance. The remaining student body therefore has become a self-selecting group, with relatively limited support available for what we might term 'non-standard' students. It is hard to see how a student with Down Syndrome might thrive in such a system once at upper secondary level, for example, even though such students are sometimes considered potentially capable of sitting some GCSE examinations in the UK. Yet the European Schools System is meant to be a comprehensive system, suggesting a discrepancy between the original inclusive intention, and current policies and practices.

We have no available data on student sexuality, so it may be that just as gender is not a particular issue for the European Schools, sexuality may not be either. A lack of the usual sites of discriminatory practice, such as compulsory school uniforms, may contribute to a sense of tolerance and inclusion as far as different identities are concerned.

The student body of the European Schools is primarily white, as one might expect given the geographical and historic basis of the European Union, although there is some privileging of certain kinds of ethnicity over others. An example of this is the fact that Islam appears in relation to religious education, but there is no separate coverage of Judaism. Given the legacy of the Second World War, and the fact that its existence was a significant contributory factor in the founding of the European Union itself, this is surprising.

Given the social positioning of many European schools' families, it became clear throughout the course of our study that a form of 'back door' selection was evident within the system. This was achieved through firstly, having a predominance of graduate parents, and secondly an easing out of particular children at S4 (upper secondary level) who might be struggling with Science and Mathematics. In this way, social class has been conflated with notions of intelligence and academic ability, in a way that is unhelpful to those that had been rejected by a system acting in its own interests (rather than those of the wider European Union community). This is a school system located within an advanced capitalist economy where university attendance is heavily associated with meritocratic advancement. We saw this routinely acknowledged by parents and teachers, when they spoke of the competitive nature of university entry in many countries, such as the UK stratified system as well as the US college system, the French Grandes Ecoles and so on. In this way it is possible to see the social reproduction of the bureaucratic classes in action. This is linked to a socially fluid movement of families across different countries but within the same cadre of society. The notion of comparative social time also played a part here. Basil Bernstein developed a concept of the 'symbolic ruler' in which children at school were measured against each other to check their speed of relative development (Bernstein 2000). Those students in the European Schools System who develop at a different rate are often described as being 'behind' and needing to 'stay down' through repetition of school years. We also became aware of unselfconscious phraseology in documentation of 'future leaders' amongst upper secondary students, as a justification for enhanced provision and funding levels. In this regard, social status has been conflated not only with intelligence, but also with leadership qualities.

Curriculum and Higher Education Preparedness

A final aspect of progression to university that needs to be raised is that of the relationship between individual curriculum subjects, and those routinely encountered in the modern university. If we examine the European Baccalaureate as it currently stands, we see that many of the subjects take a form similar to that elsewhere in Europe in the mid-twentieth century. In this sense, subjects can be seen as fairly traditional and as such, recognised by various university systems. However within the higher education sector there have been changes in recent years in the way that subjects are grouped. We see increasing numbers of applied subjects, as well as interdisciplinary approaches to different subjects that look very different from what is on offer in the European schools. In the European schools' curriculum, upper secondary subjects are as follows:

> Art, Biology, Chemistry, Economics, Physical Education, Geography, Ancient Greek, History, ICT, Language 1, Language 2, Language 3, Language 4, Latin, Mathematics, Advanced Mathematics, Ethics and Religious Studies, Music, Other National Language, Physics, Religion and Philosophy. (Note: the situation of Latin and Greek is unusual in that it only relevant to a relatively limited number of students, such as for university entrance requirements in Greece).

Conspicuously absent are popular academic subjects such as psychology, explicit provision for non-European language such as Mandarin, Japanese and Arabic, sociology, social science, engineering, law, technology, and so on. In the light of this absence, we analysed the curricula of three leading universities to establish patterns of subject engagement, compared to the spread of subjects available for the university entrance qualification, the European Baccalaureate. Here we see the nature of the curriculum problem. At university level, traditional subjects form the minority of degree programmes available, yet within the European Schools they represent the exclusive offering to students, and this allows us to see why some students might become potentially disengaged with such a system in the absence of reform.

University College London (UCL)

The range of degrees on offer at UCL is as follows. As can be seen, many are interdisciplinary in character, or represent subjects not studied at the European schools (see Table 6.1).

University of Luxembourg

The University of Luxembourg offers the following undergraduate degrees (Bachelors). Once again, it is clear that many of the subject areas are applied or interdisciplinary (see Table 6.2).

Table 6.1 University College London Undergraduate Degrees

Anthropology (2 degrees);
Applied Medical Sciences (2 degrees);
Archaeology (6 degrees);
Architecture (3 degrees);
Arts and Sciences (2 degrees);
Biochemical Engineering and Bioprocessing (4 degrees);
Biochemistry and Biotechnology (2 degrees);
Biological Sciences (2 degrees);
Biomedical Sciences (1 degree);
Chemical Engineering (2 degrees);
Chemistry (13 degrees);
Civil and Environmental Engineering (2 degrees);
Classical World (10 degrees);
Computer Science (3 degrees);
Earth Science (9 degrees);
Economics (2 degrees);
Economics and Business (3 degrees);
Education (3 degrees);
Electronic and Electrical engineering (2 degrees);
English (1 degree);
European Languages, Culture and Society (15 degrees);
European Social and Political Studies (2 degrees);
Fine Art (2 degrees);
Geography (6 degrees);
Hebrew and Jewish Studies (5 degrees);
History (5 degrees);
History (Russian and East European) (2 degrees);
History of Art (2 degrees);
Human Sciences (2 degrees);
Law (5 degrees);
Linguistics (2 degrees);
Management Science and Innovation (4 degrees);
Mathematics (14 degrees);
Mechanical Engineering (4);
Medical Physics and Biomedical Engineering (4 degrees);
Medicine (1 degree);
Natural Sciences (2 degrees);
Neuroscience (2 degrees);
Pharmacology (2 degrees);
Pharmacy (1 degree);
Philosophy (4 degrees);
Physics and Astrophysics (6 degrees);
Political Science (1 degree);

(continued)

Table 6.1 (continued)

Politics (2 degrees);
Population Health (1 degree);
Project Management for Construction (2 degrees);
Psychology (2 degrees);
Psychology and Language Sciences (1 degree);
Russian and East European Languages and Culture (12 degrees);
Science and Technology Studies (2 degrees);
Social Sciences (2 degrees);
Statistical Science (6 degrees);
Urban Planning and Urban Studies (3 degrees).

Table 6.2 University of Luxembourg Undergraduate Degrees

Bachelor en informatique (Language of Instruction – English and French);
Bachelor en ingénierie (Language of Instruction – French and German): Filière Électrotechnique, Filière Énergie et Environnement, Filière Génie Civil (Construction), Filière Génie Civil (Urbanisme et Aménagement du Territoire), Filière Gestion de Chantiers en Europe, Filière Mécanique Générale, Filière Mécatronique, Filière Télécommunication;
Bachelor en sciences et ingénierie (Language of Instruction – English, French and German) – Filière Ingénierie (Électrotechnique, Génie civil Mécanique, Informatique), Filière Mathématiques, Filière Physique; Bachelor en Sciences de la Vie (language of Instruction – French and German) – Filière Biologie, Filière Médecine, Filière Pharmacie;
Bachelor en droit (Language of Instruction – French and English);
Bachelor en sciences économiques et de gestion (Language of Instruction – French and English);
Bachelor en gestion (Language of Instruction – French and English) – Fillère Assurances, Fillère Banques, Fillère Entreprises;
Bachelor en cultures européennes (Language of Instruction – French, English and German) – Filière English Studies, Filière Études Françaises, Filière Germanistik, Filière Histoire, Filière Philosophie;
Bachelor en psychologie (Language of Instruction – French, English and German);
Bachelor en sciences de l'éducation (Language of Instruction – French, English, German and Luxembourg);
Bachelor en sciences sociales et éducative (Language of Instruction – French and German).

University of Barcelona

In the University of Barcelona the following undergraduate degrees are being offered, and again, many are applied and/or interdisciplinary (see Table 6.3).

Table 6.3 University of Barcelona Undergraduate Degrees

Developmental and Educational Psychology;
Logic, History and the Philosophy of Science;
Physiological Sciences;
Constitutional Law and Political Science;
History of Law, Roman Law and State Ecclesiastical Law;
Pharmacy and Pharmaceutical Technology;
Organic Chemistry;
Social Psychology;
Structure and Constituents of Matter;
Catalan;
Geochemistry, Petrology and Geological Prospecting; Public Health;
Applied Mathematics and Analysis;
English and German;
Modern History;
Economic History and Institutions;
Medicine;
Plant Biology;
Cultural Anthropology and the History of America and Africa;
Latin;
Physical Geography and Regional Geographical Analysis;
Greek;
Personality, Evaluation and Psychological Treatment;
Chemistry;
Nutrition and Bromatology;
Public Relations;
Spanish;
Biochemistry and Molecular Biology;
Fundamental Physics;
Algebra and Geometry;
Economics and Business Organization;
Methods of Research and Diagnosis in Education;
Probability, Logic and Statistics;
Drawing;
Materials Science and Metallurgical Engineering;
Contemporary History;
Human Geography;
Philology;
Geodynamics and Geophysics;
Painting;
Surgery and Surgical Specializations;
Cell Biology;
Public Health, Mental Health and Perinatal Nursing;
Social Work and Social Services;
Applied Physics and Optics.

Some Concluding Thoughts

This chapter has dealt with the relationship between the European Schools and higher education progression pathways. This is more significant than just considering how students move from one to the other on the educational conveyor belt common to most eighteen year olds. Whilst superficially successful in academic terms, these same progression pathways clearly demonstrate some of the more negative aspects of the wider European Schools System. By this we mean inclusion issues, as well as the deployment of a dated curriculum structure that is becoming increasingly out of step with the offer of many other European institutions. This is something which was clear in our conversations with alumni, who described being well prepared for a different kind of degree course to that which they had ultimately experienced, with theoretical rather than applied skills at the forefront of their schooling, and language skills that did not always link closely enough to workplace needs. In addition, very small teaching groups and perhaps overly conscientious tutorial nurturing sometimes contributed to low levels of individual resilience later on. The European Schools System was built with good intentions, but the product it was delivering had become decoupled from wider society.

To the credit of the wider European schools family, it is the awareness of this situation as well as a desire for reform that is driving engagement with alternatives, combined with an extensive redrafting of its curriculum offer. In this way, they are challenging the effects of the very limited external moderation and scrutiny that has been the practice until now, which has allowed the system to become increasingly introspective over the decades. There is also a growing understanding that the current high cost, high academic attainment model, one of the most expensive in the world, has moved away from the original intentions of its founders, who emphasised inclusion rather than elitism. While internationalism has always been a clear and distinct strength of the system, in a globalised knowledge-based economy, this has started to hamper innovation in the face of an older curriculum model that emphasises traditional forms of knowledge. Current success in higher education access for European Baccalaureate graduates disguises a system under threat from changes to the external environment. In the last chapter we examine in greater detail the notion of Cosmopolitanism/Europeanism and the pedagogic arrangements that can be made for it.

Open Access This chapter is licensed under the terms of the Creative Commons Attribution 4.0 International License (http://creativecommons.org/licenses/by/4.0/), which permits use, sharing, adaptation, distribution and reproduction in any medium or format, as long as you give appropriate credit to the original author(s) and the source, provide a link to the Creative Commons license and indicate if changes were made.

The images or other third party material in this chapter are included in the chapter's Creative Commons license, unless indicated otherwise in a credit line to the material. If material is not included in the chapter's Creative Commons license and your intended use is not permitted by statutory regulation or exceeds the permitted use, you will need to obtain permission directly from the copyright holder.

7

Belonging Together: A Model for Education in a New European Age

We conclude this book by examining the values of the European Schools System and how these are and can be translated into pedagogic practices. We have already suggested that the system has a framework of values: the eight competences. The rationale, therefore, for the curriculum is and should be that it conforms to these eight competences, leading to the European Baccalaureate: communication in the mother tongue; communication in foreign languages; mathematical competence and basic competences in science and technology; digital competence; learning to learn; social and civic competences; a sense of initiative and entrepreneurship; and cultural awareness and expression. What these competences fundamentally embrace is a set of European, anti-nationalistic and cosmopolitan values, and the sense of supporting the views of marginalized students, teachers and parents in order to develop an appropriate pedagogy to allow an inclusive sense of citizenship (Banks 1997, 1998, 2004). What has happened all too frequently in the history of the European Schools System is the development of a set of inclusive values that can genuinely address the problems of modern education systems, and at the same time, a set of pedagogical values and strategies that are not fit for this important purpose.

In the first place we need to address those theories that, as educationalists, allow us to provide education in a diversity of contexts, recognise the citizenship of minority groups and promote democracy. This means that policy-makers within the system need to address issues such as citizenship, human rights, utopian perspectives, cosmopolitanism and democracy in a pedagogic context. Cosmopolitanism has a long lineage, having roots in ancient Greek philosophy and the European Enlightenment. The cosmopolitan perspective is an ideal that 'combines a commitment to humanist principles and norms, an assumption of human equality, with a recognition of difference, and indeed a celebration of diversity' (Kaldor 2003: 19).

Though emblematic of the ancient Greek Enlightenment, the political culture portrayed in the writings of Plato and Aristotle is not cosmopolitan. Here, a man (and the citizen here is thought of as exclusively male) identifies himself first and foremost as a citizen of a particular polis, and his allegiance is to a set of institutions and a body of people, rather than to any supra-national or worldly entity. This allegiance required him to defend the polis from attacks, abide by decisions made by its democratic institutions, and contribute to the common good of its people. In addition, the virtuous citizen was not expected to share with or serve those living outside the city walls. The good Athenian was privileged over the foreigner, and in a similar way, the freeman had rights and responsibilities that were superior to those held and discharged by women, children and slaves. This is a limited form of cosmopolitanism.

However, Platonism and Aristotelianism do not represent the totality of ancient Greek thought; and there were certainly many Greek thinkers who embraced some of the tenets of cosmopolitanism. Xenophobic beliefs and practices, though endorsed by many in the ancient Greek polis, were not uniformly accepted or advocated. Yet even as Plato and Aristotle were writing, other Greeks were enthusiastically arguing for forms of cosmopolitanism and refusing to accept that the foreigner should be demonized. Traveling intellectuals, such as Herodotus and Thales, argued for a way of life that was both enlightened in an intellectual sense and respected the rights and freedoms of humanity. Socrates, too, was sensitive to this sense of universalism, or at least this is how Plato understood his thinking. Socrates was concerned with a notion of self-

and other-examination, with these examinations being understood in both a personal and political sense, extending to Athenians and foreigners alike.

Stoic cosmopolitanism in its various guises was enormously persuasive throughout the Greco-Roman world. Although the term cosmopolitan (κοσμοπολίτης, literally, world-citizen), originated earlier than the Stoic philosophers, it was these philosophers who gave meaning to the term, even if that meaning is somewhat different from the way it is used now. As early as 340 BC Diogenes the Cynic (1925a) described himself as 'a citizen of the world' (in Greek, kosmopolites), and Antiphon (1965), a little later, wrote that 'by nature we are all constituted alike in all things, both barbarians and greeks. ... This can be seen by consideration of those things which are essential by nature to all men. In these things no barbarian is set apart from us, nor any Greek. For we all breathe into the air through mouth and nostrils ...'. Zeno (1925b), in his *Republic*, was reported by Plutarch as saying: '(m)oreover, the much-admired Republic of Zeno, the founder of the Stoic sect, may be summed up in this one main principle: that all the inhabitants of this world of ours should not live differentiated by their respective rules of justice into separate cities and communities, but that we should consider all men to be of one community and one polity, and that we should have a common life and an order common to us all, even as a herd that feeds together and shares the pasturage of a common field'. Stoic philosophers later offered a dual notion of citizenship, that of the local polis, city-state or nation complemented by that of the kosmos (universe or world). This is redolent of the modern notion of layered citizenship, embracing local and global elements, including a notion of Europeanism. This sense of common humanity, reflected in our ability to reason, was later seen as a principle of natural law, and the philosopher, John Locke (2007 [1689]), at a much later point in time, used it to develop a notion of a universal code of justice and an idea that human beings have inalienable rights regardless of what governments said and did.

Stoic cosmopolitanism made many people more receptive to the cosmopolitan ideal and thus contributed greatly to its widespread influence. Cosmopolitanism slowly emerged as a key theme of the European Enlightenment, exemplified in the writings of the renowned international scholar, Erasmus of Rotterdam. Erasmus explicitly drew on ancient cosmopolitan texts to argue for the ideal of a world-wide peace. The emphasis here was on the indivisibility of human beings in contrast to dividing peoples into states, religions, races, castes or any other grouping, and then describing these divisions as natural kinds. Erasmus pleaded in effect for national and religious tolerance (cf. *Querela Pacis*, Erasmus Desiderius 2017).

There were many reasons for the emergence of cosmopolitan ideas during the European enlightenment: the increasing growth of capitalism and world-wide trade; empire building and the early manifestations of globalisation; the exploration and settlement of hitherto inaccessible parts of the world; the renewed interest in Hellenistic philosophy (though this was limited to Ancient Greek speakers); and the emergence of a notion of human rights with a focus on human reason. Many intellectuals at this time gave their allegiance to membership of an informal network of transnational thinkers, rather than to a nation state, or city or polis. This prepared them to think in terms other than those of states and peoples and adopt a cosmopolitan perspective. Under the influence of the American Revolution, and especially during the first years of the French Revolution, cosmopolitanism as an idea underwent a revival. The 1789 declaration of human rights grew out of cosmopolitan modes of thinking and reinforced them in turn.

These early forms of globalised thinking and globalised practices took a number of forms. Globalising processes, in so far as they have real effects (we also have to take account of vernacular pressures), work in two ways: firstly, national governments operate within global markets and therefore fashion their policies to fit this agenda or to exploit it; and secondly, national governments are subject to pressure from forces outside their jurisdiction that influence their policies and practices. Further to this, the success of any intervention or experiment (by the state or another body operating outside the state), or at least the path it takes, is not just determined by the system into which it is being introduced but also by the type of intervention that is being made. Interventions and experiments are time sequenced, so that they are likely to have different effects at different moments in the history of a country or continent such as Europe.

Globalisation works in a number of distinctive ways, and this means that social objects and social mechanisms operate in open systems and therefore have particular properties, including generative causal powers. McLaren and Farahmandpur (2001), for example, have suggested that globalisation is a cultural phenomenon and can only be recognised by changes to the forms these cultural phenomena take. So that instead of distinct national forms and identities, there is a cross-fertilisation of ideas, a creation of hybrid cultural forms, an homogenisation of culture, and a standardisation of cultural products. This leads to a sense of cultural sameness or conformism. Globalisation also points to the establishment of globalised markets and global consumer identities.

A second manifestation is that of the expanding nature of capitalization. This can take a number of forms. For example, it may be spatial as capital seeks to fill all the possible social, geographical and physical spaces available to it. Capitalization may also expand through the invention of new types of commodity. And the third form it might take is where capital expands through what might be called intensification; it deepens and develops its influence in the world.

In the eighteenth century, the terms, 'cosmopolitanism' and 'world citizenship', were not thought of as belonging to coherent frameworks of ideas, but rather they pointed to an attitude of open-mindedness and impartiality. A cosmopolitan was someone who did not subscribe to a particular religious or political authority. The term was sometimes used to refer to a person who had a network of international contacts, or felt at home in the world, rather than in the nation or locality in which they were born. In this sense the *Encyclopédie* suggested that a cosmopolitan was a 'man of no fixed abode, or a man who is nowhere a stranger'. The Encyclopédie, or dictionnaire raisonné des sciences, des arts et des métiers (Encyclopaedia, or a Systematic Dictionary of the Sciences, Arts, and Crafts) was an attempt by leading Enlightenment figures to represent a new way of thinking, as is evidenced by Denis Diderot (1751–1772) argument that the Encyclopédie's aim was to 'change the way people think'. As the editor, he wanted to collect together all the world's knowledge and present it in a value-free and impartial form.

The authors of the various entries to the Encyclopédie drew on the Stoic tradition to formulate an Enlightenment version of cosmopolitanism, which gave precedence to a positive moral ideal in the form of a universal human community. This community is characterized by the principles of freedom, equality and lawful behaviour. These common laws, however, are moral laws grounded in reason. Immanuel Kant (1992) also developed the concept of cosmopolitan law, suggesting a third sphere of public law, in addition to constitutional law and international law, in which both states and individuals have rights, and where individuals have these rights as citizens of the earth rather than as citizens of particular states. Global migratory movements have brought about a situation where national citizenship is often exclusionary. However, as John Dewey noted, the identification of citizenship with the powerful discourse of nationality occurred at a specific point in history, the late nineteenth century, when imperialism flourished and democracy was reserved for a minority. In addition, Dewey recognized that cosmopolitanism is a learned perspective. Education can develop the capacity of people to identify with fellow human beings irrespective of national boundaries and develop what Appiah (2007: 82) calls 'a concern for strangers'. The European Schools System has embraced this sense of cosmopolitan identity, though its founders understood it as a European ideal and perhaps more importantly, as a pedagogic process.

Learning Environments

Acquiring a cosmopolitan identity (and certainly a European one) is a learned activity and requires the development of appropriate learning mechanisms in specialised environments, such as in the European School System, and this calls for an engagement with learning and learning environments. Theoretical and contextual considerations impact, then, on how elements of teaching and learning are realised. Acknowledging this allows the identification of a number of learning models: assessment for learning, observation, coaching, goal-clarification, mentoring, peer learning, simulation, instruction, concept-formation, reflection, meta-cognitive learning, problem solving, and practice. And each of these in turn is underpinned by a particular theory of learning. What this means is that any model of learning that is employed is constructed in relation to particular views of how we can know the world and what it is. These models or learning sets (and this includes feedback mechanisms of a particular kind) give different emphases to the various elements of a learning process.

The first of these models is the assessment for learning model. Assessment for learning can be presented as five key strategies and one cohering idea. The five key strategies are: engineering effective classroom discussions, questions, and learning tasks; clarifying and sharing learning intentions and criteria for success; providing feedback that moves learners forward; activating students as the owners of their own learning; and activating students as instructional resources for one another (Wiliam and Thompson 2008). And the cohering idea is that evidence about student learning is used to adapt instruction to better meet learning needs; in other words, teaching is adaptive to the student's learning needs and evidence from the assessments is used by teachers, learners, or their peers to improve instruction (ibid.).

An important aspect of this model is the active engagement of the learner in the learning process as both an initiator and user of feedback. The key then is the relationship between assessment (designed as formative and developmental) and learning. In this sense feedback is on-going and an integral part of assessment. The assessment for learning movement has been criticised on three grounds: the focus on formative assessment has inevitably marginalised other learning elements; as a result, some of the strategies are both misunderstood and consequently misapplied, for example, peer learning does not amount to asking students to make quantitative judgements about their colleagues' work in relation to a set of criteria; and the reductive process for the purposes of quantifying and comparing results may have led to a distorted understanding of the process of learning.

The second learning set is an observation model. Here the teacher displays the action which the learner is required to imitate in the classroom, and then later in the context of application. There are three principal types: a live model involving a demonstration or acting out of the behaviours to be learnt; a verbal instructional model where this comprises descriptions and explanations of behaviours; and a symbolic model, examples of which are scenarios and expressive performances. These are stimuli for learning. The learning skills required of the learner are: observing a performance by the teacher, whether this comprises live modelling, verbal instruction or symbolic modelling; comparing the performance with an embodied form of that display already held by the learner; adjusting their current construct through modification or substitution; practice by the learner whilst being supported within the artificial environment; practice by the learner without support within the artificial environment; transferring the skill to the real environment whilst being supported; and consolidation without support through use in the real environment (cf. Bandura 1977). This model is underpinned by a cognitivist theory of learning.

The third of these is a coaching model. Here the focus is on a series of steps: modelling by the expert; coaching whilst the learner practices; scaffolding where the learner is supported during the initial stages with that support gradually being withdrawn as the learner becomes more proficient (coaching here involves the teacher in identifying for the learner deviations from the model in the performance of the learner, and then supporting the learner as they make attempts to correct this performance); articulation by the learner of that process; reflection on those processes and comparison with the expert's reasons for action; and exploration where the learner undertakes the various activities without support (cf. Collins et al. 1989). Coaching can be seen as a one-to-one activity, or as a collective exercise within a community of practice. This model better fits a socio-cultural theory of learning.

A fourth model involves clarifying and sharing learning intentions and criteria for success with the student over a period of time. To this end, teachers provide learners with explicit statements and explanations about the instructional objectives in a lesson or series of lessons (Zimmerman and Schunk 2011). Goal clarity has three learner-focused dimensions: explanations about how they are expected to perform the tasks assigned to them; opportunities for them to grasp what is expected of them; and reflections about their capacity as self-directed learners in the completion of the task. This mechanism comprises a number of processes: identifying the standard and interpreting its meaning; providing a description with the learner of their mastery of that standard, which should allow the identification of weaknesses in their capacity and the means for ameliorating these weaknesses; record-keeping for further identification of the learner's current capability; reflection on this and the identification of the means of improving; and a meta-reflective record of progress in the curriculum (Meece et al. 2006).

A fifth model is mentoring. This supports the informal transmission of content knowledge, social capital or psychosocial resources. It is usually conducted face-to-face and involves a relationship between two people, one of whom is considered to have greater knowledge, wisdom or experience. Five possible mentoring techniques have been identified (cf. Aubrey and Cohen 1995): supporting the learner and taking part in the same activity and learning side-by-side with them; preparing the learner for the future even if they are not ready or able to learn what is being offered to them in the present; catalysing learning so that it provokes a different way of thinking, a change in identity or a re-ordering of values; showing through personal example; and finally, helping and supporting the learner in reflecting back on their previous learning. The terms, coaching and mentoring, are often used synonymously, however, important distinctions between these two approaches can be identified. In distinguishing between these two terms, Clutterbuck and Megginson (2005) identify three specific differences in terms of emphasis: time-scale, approach and context. For example, coaching is focused on performance change whilst mentoring is focused on managing elements of the life-course; and coaching is focused on the immediate context whereas mentoring involves enlarging a learner's networks. In addition, coaching is typically seen as of much shorter duration and in response to a specific goal, whereas mentoring considers immediate issues as part of long-term change. Both mentoring and coaching are about achieving change, and place a strong emphasis on the development of learner self-regulation through the use of appropriate tools, such as critical reflection and scaffolded support.

A sixth model of learning is peer learning. The other forms of learning comprise unequal relations between the teacher and the learner. Here the assumption is made that the learning relationship is between equals, and thus a different form of learning is implied. Examples of this type of learning include: being offered emotional support if learning proves to be difficult and this is always a better form of support if given by someone who is going through the same learning process; dyadic performance confrontations, where learning is provoked by confrontational exchanges between learners so that each individual can test their theories, ideas and constructs against those held by other learners engaging in the same type of learning; pair-problem-solving, where learning is enabled through cooperation between two learners of roughly equal standing, so that in a problem-solving exercise, better solutions are forthcoming because there are two problem-solvers rather than one; reciprocal peer tutoring, where non-expert tutoring between equals has the advantage of each person being able to make their own evaluation of the advice being offered unencumbered by status or hierarchy; and scripted cooperative dyads, where peer engagement is focused on the joint production of a script, artefact, performance or text with the advantage that alternative and new interpretations/readings are forthcoming (cf. Falchikov 2001).

A seventh model of learning involves simulation. Simulation is a reproduction of an event or activity, conducted outside the environment in which that event or activity usually takes place. Simulations can be produced through computer games, role-plays, scenarios, presentations and affective and conceptual modelling. The purpose of this learning process is to simulate a real event, and this is to allow the person or persons taking part in that simulation to explore it, to experiment within it, to understand the process, to begin the process of internalisation, to experience albeit in a limited way the emotions and feelings that would normally accompany the experience in real-life, and fundamentally, to allow learning to take place through trial and error and making mistakes in safe situations, which do not have the consequences they would have in real-life situations. Simulations compress time and remove extraneous detail. They are immersive learning experiences, where skills and performances can be enhanced in a way that is not possible outside the simulation. Simulation is an element of learning that has implications for all the theories of learning that have been identified above. As a consequence of the simulative effect the pedagogic object is different in some fundamental respects from the original learning object.

In the instructional model the teacher needs to: gain the attention of the group of learners; inform the learners of the objectives of the learning exercise; stimulate recall of prior learning amongst the group of learners, so that the new information is related productively to previous and current learning; present content to the learner; implement appropriate scaffolding processes; stimulate a performance by the learner; provide feedback to the learner which is a comment on their performance and allows corrective action to take place; and evaluate the corrected performance (cf. Gagné 1985). Cognitivist theorists of learning commonly advocate instructional models of learning, because of the emphasis they place on invariant knowledge objects and schematic adjustments to accommodate these objects.

A concept-formation learning process focuses on the re-forming of the conceptual schema held by the learner and one version of it is underpinned by an inferentialist pragmatist philosophy (cf. Brandom 2000). This positions knowledge and knowledge-development within networks of meaning, which are social in character and historical in origin. Learning is complex and potentially rich and rewarding, where the learner is presented with a mass of information, ideas, and opinions from a number of different sources (i.e. books, articles, lectures, seminars, emails, eseminars, personal communications and so on). What the learner does is shape this mass of information, and this shaping can take a number of different forms: partial shaping, complete shaping, discarding with no replacement, confusion, on-going, going backwards and forwards and so on. Shaping takes place against a scholarly background; aspects of which may or may not be implicit and where some but not all of its aspects can be surfaced for deliberation. Conceptual learning is irredeemably social, embedded, and selective. So the learner has to absorb some of the ideas they are presented with and discard or partially discard others. Again, this notion of concept-formation has elements of socio-cultural theories of learning.

Reflection is a seminal form of learning. It has been variously described as critical reflection, reflective practice, reflective thinking and reflexivity. Whereas some see these terms as interchangeable and as having similar meanings, others have sought to differentiate between different types and levels of reflective activity (cf. Black and Plowright 2010). Not all reflection is critical reflection. Bolton (2010: 13) defined reflection (single loop activity) as 'an in-depth consideration of events or situations outside of oneself: solitary or with critical support', and reflexivity as a double loop process which includes reflection and reflexivity and is focused on 'finding strategies to question our own attitudes, thought processes, values, assumptions, prejudices and habitual actions, to strive to understand our complex roles with others'. Wilson and Demetriou (2007) differentiate between three types of reflective practice: intensive action reflection which is seen as tacit, implicit and occurring on a daily basis in practice where individuals use intuitive tacit knowledge to inform practice (reflection-in-action); reactive or reflective learning (knowledge of action) involving immediate reactive reflection on events that have already taken place; and deliberative reflection (knowledge for action) involving the conscious management of thoughts and activity and the deliberate setting aside of time to ensure that judgements are based on a deep understanding of a particular issue.

Meta-cognitive learning refers to learners' awareness of their own knowledge and their ability to understand, control, and manipulate their own cognitive processes. Most meta-cognitive processes can be placed within three categories (cf. Harris and Graham 1999). The first is metamemorisation. This refers to the learners' awareness of their own memory systems and their ability to deploy strategies for using their memories effectively. The second is meta-comprehension. This refers to the learners' ability to monitor the degree to which they understand information being communicated to them, to recognize failures to comprehend, and to employ repair strategies. And the third is self-regulation. This term refers to the learner's ability to make adjustments in their own learning processes. The concept of self-regulation overlaps with meta-memorisation and meta-comprehension; its focus is on the capacity of the learners themselves to monitor their own learning (without external stimuli or persuasion) and to act independently. These regulatory processes may be highly automated, making articulation of them difficult for the learner.

A problem-solving approach is where the learner finds out for themselves rather than being given answers to problems. The learner is required to engage in a series of interrogative processes with regards to texts, people and objects in the environment, and come up with solutions to problems. The learner is also required to use the skills of information retrieval, information synthesis and analysis, and knowledge organization. The learner may come up with inadequate, incorrect and faulty syntheses and analyses. However, this is acceptable because the learning resides in the process rather than the end product. Problem-solving learning involves the learner in judging their own work against a curriculum standard and engaging in meta-processes of learning, that is, understandings about processes related to their own learning; the development of learning pathways; the utilisation of formative assessment processes; the development of personal learning strategies; and the internalisation of the curriculum.

Finally, there is practice. Practice is the act of rehearsing a behaviour over and over again, or engaging in an activity again and again. This reinforces, enhances and deepens the learning associated with the behaviour or activity. Choosing between these models depends on the nature and constitution of the learning object; in other words, the former is logically dependent on the latter. It also depends on the choice of learning theory that is made. Thus, the European cosmopolitan ideal, embraced by the European School System, has to be translated into a set of concrete pedagogic practices that do not in any way distort or neglect its underlying principles, and this involves making choices between the learning models discussed above: assessment for learning, observation, coaching, goal-clarification, mentoring, peer learning, simulation, instruction, concept-formation, reflection, meta-cognitive learning, problem solving, and practice.

Pedagogic Knowledge

Knowledge is transformed at the pedagogic site, so it is possible to suggest that qualities such as: the simulation of the learning object, the representational mode of the object, its degree and type of amplification, control in the pedagogic relationship, progression or its relations with other learning objects (i.e. curriculum integration), the type of pedagogic text, relations with other people in the learning process, the organization of time (temporal relations) and types of feedback mechanism are fundamental components of this pedagogic transformation. What this means is that in the learning process, the learning object takes a new form as a result of changes to its properties: simulation, representation, amplification, control, integration, textual form, relations with other people, time and feedback.

The first of these is the degree and type of simulation. In a simulation a new medium is chosen which gives the learning object a new form, these media being virtual, graphic, enumerative, enactive, symbolic or oral. Indeed, depending on the new form, there is a distance between the original object and the mediated object, and this can vary in strength. This doesn't mean that the object is better or less well represented in its new form, only that it takes on a new guise; it is pedagogically formed. And this means that its potential impact is likely to be different. A simulation might involve, for practical purposes, a computer representation of something in nature that cannot be experienced by the learner. Inevitably, the elements of the object and the relations between those elements are both reduced and changed in the simulation; and what this means is that any reaction or response to the object by a learner is influenced by its new media as well as the shape and form it now assumes. The response is always to the mediated object. And the implication of this is that the pedagogical relation between the learner and the world is never direct but is realised through the mediated object, with the process of knowing the unmediated object a retroductive one ('from a description and analysis of concrete phenomena to a reconstruction of the basic conditions for these phenomena to be as they are' – Bhaskar 2010: 34), although this may be understood in a different way by the learner.

A second property is the type of truth criterion that the knowledge-constructor adopts. David Bridges (1999) itemised five conceptions of truth: truth as correspondence, truth as coherence, truth as what works, truth as consensus and truth as warranted belief. This property comprises a determination of the relationship between knowledge and the world, though it should never be assumed that this relationship is straightforward, linear or easily understood.

A third property, which is subject to transformation during the learning process, is amplification. Amplification is a central term in rhetoric, and stands for all the ways that an argument, explanation, or description can be expanded and enriched. In addition, amplification refers to the capacity of the pedagogic object to increase in size, in extent, or in effect, as by the addition of extra material. The use of a microscope in a science laboratory, or the use of the internet to extend the reach of the learning object, or the taking of a deliberate and alternative position from the accepted norm for the sake of debate or to further the argument, but always to deepen the learning process, are typical examples of amplification.

A fourth property is control in the pedagogic relationship. Framing refers to the message system of pedagogy (cf. Bernstein 2000). Do teachers and pupils control its content, its organisation, how it is sequenced, and so on? A syllabus with rigid topics, to be completed in a predetermined order, within a specified time, is strongly framed. Weak framing occurs when the teacher is able to select topics on the basis of some principle, and organise the sequence and pacing of material according to pupil readiness. Two control pathways can be identified. The first refers to the relationship between teacher and learner *and* the curriculum organisers of knowledge (these organising processes may be formal or informal), so a teacher or facilitator of the message system has either a restricted or extended control over the way it is received in the pedagogic setting. The second refers to the relationship between the teacher *and* learner and again this refers to the amount of control either one or the other has over the constitution of the message that is central to the pedagogic or learning process. Clearly, in this last case the one varies in relation to variation in the other.

A fifth property is curriculum integration or the types of relations between other learning objects. Progression is one manifestation of these relations. Curriculum standards, or learning objects, are written at different levels of difficulty. Most forms of progression between levels or grades in curricula round the world are based on a notion of extension, i.e. at level one a student should be able to do this or that, at level two the student is expected to be able to do more of this or that, and at level three the student is expected to be able to do even more of this or that. However, there are other forms of progression between designated knowledge sets, skills and dispositions besides extension. Indeed, some knowledge sets, skills and dispositions cannot be appropriately placed at some lower-level or even some higher-level grades. For example, many countries round the world have chosen not to start formal reading processes until at least seven years of age, and thus reading does not feature in the curriculum standards at pre-primary levels in these countries.

Fogarty (1991) has identified ten models of curriculum integration and these range from strongly classified and strongly framed curricula, as in the traditional or fragmented approach, *to* weakly classified and weakly framed networked approaches to curriculum planning (cf. Bernstein 1985). Between the two extremes: traditional or fragmented and networked approaches, she identifies eight other points on the continuum: connected, nested, sequenced, shared, webbed, threaded, integrated and immersed. Each of these forms of integration can only be understood in relation to their position on this continuum and in relation to how they approximate to one or the other of the end points of the continuum.

Finally, pace of learning is important, i.e. the pace at which a student works in completing a learning activity, or the pace at which they are expected to work against some norm, i.e. the average or mean of a population. Pace can be understood as a performative construct so that it is not meant to provide an empirical description of how a person has performed but is designed to act as a stimulus to increase the pace of learning for the general population; it thus has an explicit normative function.

A sixth property is the constitution of the task given to the learner in the pedagogic setting. As we suggested in Chap. 2, there is a range of learning tasks or activities that take place in classrooms, such as: working with other people, individual study, sharing, debating, playing games and so forth. Learning tasks have a number of constituent elements and how they differ in kind allows us to determine and identify these different elements: media of expression, the logic of this mediated expression, its fit with a learning model, its assessment mode, and its relation to real-life settings. Media of expression include: oral, graphic, pictorial and enumerative modes. Each of these media has an encompassing logic to them, so that a task which requires a written response to a request is of a different order as a learning experience to one which requires an oral response. A further component of a pedagogic task or activity is the mode of assessment that inheres in it, with these modes of assessment being understood broadly as formative or summative. Finally, there is the authenticity of the task and this refers to whether the task relates to real-life settings or not, or to the degree to which it does this.

The activity or learning task has a logical relationship with the learning model being employed. Frequently there is a mismatch between them so the task or activity (i.e. an oral response to a question, a written analysis of a text, a reading exercise, an argumentative response, a feedback loop and so forth) and the type of learning model that is being adopted are incompatible. For example, a metacognitive exercise that is focused on propositional knowledge rather than process knowledge would be inappropriate. A dialogic peer-learning exercise that asked each participant to grade each other's work on a five-point scale again would be inconsonant. Feedback that failed to engage the learner in a conversation would not work.

Questioning, for example, sets up a choice situation between a finite range of possible answers. The type of answer that can be given legitimately has to be implicit in the grammar of the question, both in its form and content. For example, open-ended questions offer an infinite range of answers; that is, the restricting and enabling quality in the question is weakly formulated. What this means is that there is a greater range of possible answers to the problem. This has to be qualified in the sense that some questions by virtue of their propositional content have a greater facility for generating appropriate answers; whereas other questions have fewer possibilities for generating appropriate answers. However, this doesn't nullify the original proposition, which is that the form a question takes, placing this on an open-ended to closed-ended continuum, restricts or enables the types of correct answers that can be given to that question to different degrees. The reason for designating both an enabling and restricting function is to indicate that any action performed by an individual is located in discursive and material contexts and that these contexts exert an influence on the action itself.

A seventh property is the relationship between the learner and other people in the pedagogic setting. One way of characterising the relationship between the person, text, object in nature, particular array of resources, artefact, allocation of a role or function to a person, or sensory object *and* the learner is by determining its strength along a continuum ranging from a diffuse mode to a concentrated mode. What this means is that the message being conveyed is embedded in a relationship between the stimulus and recipient, which is either diffuse or concentrated, or could be placed on a continuum between them. An example of a diffuse strategy is an instructional mode of learning where the stimulus is being shared by a number of people. An example of a concentrated strategy is a one-to-one coaching relationship. What are the possible effects of these two types of learning? Since the relationship is both from the catalyst to the learner or learners and also from the learner or learners to the catalyst then this is going to influence the type of message received by the learner. We model the world as a sequence of messages passing from one to the other. The stimulus is clearly of a certain type. These are message conveyance systems or processes of semiotic transmission that operate with a particular stimulus denied to the learner if the stimulus for learning is different.

Learning is always embedded in temporal arrangements of one type or another. A curriculum is an arrangement of time given to different items of knowledge, so any learning episode is going to be embedded in these arrangements of time. These eight properties of the learning environment means that there is potentially a large range of possible environments since there is considerable variation within each dimension and in most cases variation in one dimension is independent of variation in the others. Finally, there are feedback mechanisms and again there is variation in this element.

Feedback is a systemic property (in the case we are considering here this is the learning process or system) and broadly consists of two types: feedback as it operates in closed systems and feedback as it operates in open systems. Hattie and Timperley (2007) use assessment feedback as a general concept to categorise definitions and types of feedback using the following dimensions: role, type, foci, meaning and function. Functionally, feedback has a scaffolding form and aims to bridge the gap between the level achieved by an individual learner and a normative level, which is subsequently used to amend that gap. Hannafin et al. (1993) distinguish between task, strategic and affective feedback. Task feedback is defined as providing activities that clarify or reinforce aspects of the learning task. Strategic feedback comprises diagnostic-prescriptive, performance, management, and process activities. Affective feedback is understood as a process of engaging learners through eliciting and sustaining their interest and engagement. Hattie and Timperley's (2007) four-fold model of levels of feedback (task, process, self-regulation and self) is an extension of this.

Black and Wiliam (1998) distinguish between directive (what needs to be changed) and facilitative (what processes can guide the learner to make those revisions to their work) types of feedback. Nelson and Schunn

(2009), in developing this framework, identify three broad types: motivational, where the intention is to influence the beliefs of the learner and their willingness to participate in the learning activities; reinforcing, where the aim is to reward or to punish specific behaviours; and informational, where the purpose is to change the performance of the learner in a particular direction. They point to the importance of being able to develop knowledge through a transfer of learning so that it is applicable in new contexts. Thus feedback is understood as multi-functional in relation to different learning environments, the needs of the learner, the purpose of the task and the particular relation feedback has to the learning theory being employed. A directive approach to feedback fits better a cognitivist perspective where it is understood as corrective with the expert providing information to the passive recipient. Alternatively, facilitative feedback identifies more closely with a socio-constructivist view where feedback is seen as a process that takes place within a learning environment, without determining what those understandings will be. Significantly, these two perspectives should be seen as reinforcing rather than as opposite ends of a continuum. The socio-constructivist view is highlighted in the need to see feedback as an integral and iterative part of the learning context and within formative assessment frameworks that emphasise interactions between teachers, pupils and subjects within communities of practice. Furthermore, within a co-constructivist approach, it is also accepted that the teacher learns from the student through dialogue and participation in a range of shared experiences (cf. Lave and Wenger 1998). Within such environments, feedback is understood as iterative, adaptive and dynamic, with different learners receiving different types of feedback and this varies at different stages of the learning process, though this principle is sometimes neglected in classrooms in European system schools.

Concluding Thoughts

The European Schools Network has existed since the European Economic Community (EEC) was founded in 1953. The system has its own rules in terms of enrolment, funding and management, as well as its own curriculum. It was first created as an instrument to meet the educational needs of the children of the civil servants working in Luxembourg for the then newly formed European Union. The different stakeholders (i.e. parents, institution officials, civil servants and policy-makers) reached an agreement that these children should have the opportunity to be educated in their mother tongue, as well as having the same standard of education as their national classmates in their home countries.

It is important to remind ourselves that mother-tongue communication is more than a competence to be acquired but fulfills a cultural role at the very heart of the European Schools' project (from Jean Monnet's '…Without ceasing to look to their own lands with love and pride…' to being embodied in the First Objective and First Principle of the Schools.) The first principle of the European Schools System is to safeguard the 'primacy of the students' mother tongue' (L1), and the first objective of the European School System is to 'give students' confidence in their own cultural identity, the bedrock for their development as European citizens'.

The European schools' curriculum is generally of a fragmented or traditional type; and what we mean by this is that there are strong and clear boundaries between the different subjects. Our suggestion in this book is that in order to genuinely take into account the needs of students faced with the demands of the modern world; to conform to the accepted and logical principles of curriculum design; to be relevant, coherent, comprehensive, and allow breadth of study for all students in the system; to guarantee in the last two years, leading to the European Baccalaureate, a general education around the eight key competences for lifelong learning; and to impact favourably on specific groups, such as students without a language section, students with special educational needs, students with more than one national language and small language sections; then, existing subject boundaries need to be reduced and subject integration and networked approaches to curriculum need to be adopted.

If reform in the European Schools is to be truly valuable, it must go beyond arcane issues relating to institutions and structures, assessment processes, subject allocations and resourcing, and linguistic issues. It must take a braver moral position that has relevance for society as a whole, even setting the tone for wider debates where it can. The changes that have already been made, and those that are being considered, might seem as though they are a reaction to internal conditions, but they are actually rooted in a pressing need to consider issues relating to learners and their contemporary social identity. For this reason, it is important to ensure not only that the European Schools have an internal sense of common purpose, but also that this relates to changes in society going on outside their immediate learning environment. Only if this is achieved can a wide range of students receive a truly valuable education fit to meet individual, societal and global needs.

Open Access This chapter is licensed under the terms of the Creative Commons Attribution 4.0 International License (http://creativecommons.org/licenses/by/4.0/), which permits use, sharing, adaptation, distribution and reproduction in any medium or format, as long as you give appropriate credit to the original author(s) and the source, provide a link to the Creative Commons license and indicate if changes were made.

The images or other third party material in this chapter are included in the chapter's Creative Commons license, unless indicated otherwise in a credit line to the material. If material is not included in the chapter's Creative Commons license and your intended use is not permitted by statutory regulation or exceeds the permitted use, you will need to obtain permission directly from the copyright holder.

References

Allemann-Ghionda, C. (2012) 'Can Intercultural Education Contribute to Equal Opportunities?', *Studi Emigrazione/Migration Studies*, XLIX, 186: 215–27.

Ansell, C. (2000) 'The Networked Polity: Regional Development in Western Europe', *Governance*, 13, 2: 279–91.

Antiphon (1965) 'On Truth, Oxyrhynchus Papyri, xi, no. 1364, fragment 1, quoted in Donald Kagan (ed.), *Sources in Greek Political Thought from Homer to Polybius, Sources in Western Political Thought*, A. Hacker, gen. ed., New York: Free Press.

Appiah, A. (1997) 'Cosmopolitan Patriots', *Critical Inquiry*, 23, 3: 617–39.

Appiah, K. (2007) Cosmopolitanism: Ethics in a World of Strangers, London: Penguin.

Argyris, C. (2010) *Organizational Traps: Leadership, Culture, Organizational Design*, Oxford: Oxford University Press.

Aubrey, B. and Cohen, P. (1995) *Working Wisdom: Timeless Skills and Vanguard Strategies for Learning Organizations*, San Francisco: Jossey Bass.

Baker, C. (2011) *Foundations of Bilingual Education and Bilingualism* (5th edition), Clevedon, UK: Multilingual Matters.

Ball, S. (2006) *Education Policy and Social Class: The Selected Works of Stephen J. Ball*, London: Routledge.

Bandura, A. (1977) *Social Learning Theory*, New York: General Learning Press.
Banks, J. (2007) *An Introduction to Multicultural Education*, London: Pearson.
Banks, J. A. (1997) *Educating Citizens in a Multicultural Society*, New York: Teachers College Press.
Banks, J. A. (1998) 'The Lives and Values of Researchers: Implications for Educating Citizens in a Multi-cultural Society', *Educational Researcher*, 27, 11: 4–17.
Banks, J. A. (2004) 'Preface', in J. Banks (ed.), *Diversity and Citizenship Education: Global Perspectives*, San Francisco: Jossey-Bass, pp. xix–xxv.
Banks, J. A. (2006) *Race, Culture and Education: The Selected Works of James A. Banks*, New York: Routledge.
Banks, J. A. (2009) 'Diversity and Citizenship Education in Multicultural Nations', *Multicultural Education Review*, 1, 1: 1–28.
Banks, J. A. and McGee, C. A. (1989) *Multicultural Education*. Needham Heights, MA: Allyn & Bacon.
Baetens Beardsmore, H. (1993) *The European School Model*, Clevedon: Multilingual Matters.
Baetens Beardsmore, H. and Kohls, J. (1988) 'Immediate Pertinence in the Acquisition of Multilingual Proficiency: The European Schools', *Canadian Modern Language Review*, 44, 2: 240–60.
Bernstein, B. (1985) 'On Pedagogic Discourse', in G. Richardson (ed.), *Handbook of Theory and Research in the Sociology of Education*, London: Taylor and Francis.
Bernstein, B. (2000) *Pedagogy, Symbolic Control and Identity: Theory, Research and Critique* (Revised edition), London: Taylor and Francis.
Bernstein, B. (2002) 'From Pedagogies to Knowledges', in A. Morais, I. Neves, B. Davies, and H. Daniels (eds.), *Towards a Sociology of Pedagogy: The Contribution of Basil Bernstein to Research*, New York: Peter Lang Publishing.
Bhaskar, R. (2010) *Reclaiming Reality*, Second Edition, London and New York: Routledge.
Black, P. and Plowright, D. (2010) 'A Multidimensional Model of Reflective Learning for Professional Development', *Reflective Practice*, 11, 2: 245–58.
Black, P. and Wiliam, D. (1998) 'Inside the Black Box: Raising Standards Through Classroom Assessment', *Phi Delta Kappan*, 80, 2: 139–48.
Board of Governors (2000) *Report*, Office of Secretary General of the European Schools, https://www.eursc.eu/en.
Board of Governors (2007) *Report*, Office of Secretary General of the European Schools, https://www.eursc.eu/en.

Board of Governors (2009) *Report*, Office of Secretary General of the European Schools, https://www.eursc.eu/en.
Board of Governors (2011) *Report*, Office of Secretary General of the European Schools, https://www.eursc.eu/en.
Board of Governors (2012) *Report*, Office of Secretary General of the European Schools, https://www.eursc.eu/en.
Board of Governors, the European Schools (2013) *Accredited European Schools* Ref.: 2013-01-D-64-en-4, Brussels, Office of the Secretary-General, The European Schools.
Bolton, G. (2010) *Reflective Practice*, London: Sage.
Bonefeld, W. (1999) 'The Politics of Change: Ideology and Critique', *Common Sense: Journal of the Edinburgh Conference of Socialist Economists*, 24: 76–90.
Boud, D. and Falchikov, N. (2006) 'Aligning Assessment with Long-term Learning', *Assessment and Evaluation in Higher Education*, 31, 4: 399–413.
Bourdieu, P. and Passeron, J.-C. (1994) 'Introduction: Language and the Relationship to Language in the Teaching Situation', in P. Bourdieu, J.-C. Passeron and M. de Saint Martin (Eds.), *Academic Discourse*, Cambridge: Polity Press, pp. 1–34.
Brandom, R. (1994) *Making It Explicit: Reasoning, Representing, and Discursive Commitment*, Cambridge, MA: Harvard University Press.
Brandom, R. (2000) *Articulating Reasons: An Introduction to Inferentialism*, Cambridge, MA: Harvard University Press.
Bridges, D. (1999) 'Educational Research: Pursuit of Truth or Flight of Fancy', *British Educational Research Journal*, 25, 5: 597–616.
Brinton, D., Snow, A. and Wesche, M. (2011) *Content-Based Second Language Instruction* (5th edition), Ann Arbor: The University of Michigan Press.
Bruner, J. (1996) *The Culture of Education*, Cambridge, MA: Harvard University.
Bullock, A. (1975) *A Language for Life*, London: Department of Education and Science.
Bulmer, J. (1990) 'Becoming a European: Languages and Nationalities in a European School', *Ricerca Educativa*, 3–4.
Bulwer, J. (1995) 'European Schools: Languages for All?', *Journal of Multilingual and Multicultural Development*, 16, 6: 459–75.
Cambridge University, Department of International Examinations (2009) *Final Report on the External Evaluation of the European Baccalaureate*, Cambridge: University of Cambridge.
Cammarata, L. (2016) 'Foreign Language Education and the Development of Inquiry-Driven Learning Programs', in L. Cammarata (ed.), *Content Based*

Foreign Language Teaching: For Developing Advanced Thinking and Literacy, New York, NY: Routledge, 123–146.

Cammarata, L., Tedick, D. J. and Osborn, T. A. (2016) 'Content-Based Instruction and Curricular Reforms: Issues and Goals', in L. Cammarata (ed.), *Content-based Foreign Language Teaching: For Developing Advanced Thinking and Literacy*, New York, NY: Routledge, pp. 1–21.

Candelier, M., Camilleri-Grima, A., Castellotti, V., de Pietro, J.F., Lőrincz, I., Meißner, F.-J., Noguerol, A. and Schröder-Sura, A. (2012) *The Framework of Reference for Pluralistic Approaches to Languages and Cultures: Competences and Resources*, Graz: European Centre for Modern Languages.

Carlos, S. (2012) 'Governing Education in Europe: A 'New' Policy Space of European Schooling', *European Educational Research Journal*, 11, 4: 487–503.

Chamot, A. and O'Malley, J. (1996) 'The Cognitive Academic Language Learning Approach (CALLA): A Model for Linguistically Diverse Classrooms', *The Elementary School Journal*, 96, 3: 259–73.

Cloud, N., Genesee, F. and Hamayan, E. (2000) *Dual Language Instruction: A Handbook for Enriched Education*, Portsmouth, NH: Heinle and Heinle.

Clutterbuck, D. and Megginson, D. (2005) *Making Coaching Work – Creating a Coaching Culture*, London: Chartered Institute of Personnel and Development.

Collins, A., Brown, J. and Newman, S. (1989) 'Cognitive Apprenticeship: Teaching the Crafts of Reading, Writing, and Mathematics', in L. B. Resnick (ed.), *Knowing, Learning, and Instruction: Essays in Honour of Robert Glaser*, Hillsdale, NJ: Lawrence Erlbaum Associates, pp. 453–94.

Council of Europe (2007a) *From Linguistic Diversity to Plurilingual Education: Guide for the Development of Language Education Policies in Europe*, Strasbourg: Council of Europe. [http://www.coe.int/t/dg4/linguistic/Guide_niveau2_EN.asp, access date 24/01/2010]

Council of Europe (2007b) *The Common European Framework: Learning, Teaching, Assessment*, Strasbourg: Council of Europe. [http://www.coe.int/T/DG4/Linguistic/CADRE_EN.asp, access date 24/01/2010]

Council of Europe (2011) *Common European Framework of Reference for Languages: Learning, Teaching, Assessment*, Strasbourg: Council of Europe.

Council of Europe (2016) *Competences for Democratic Culture: Living Together as Equals in Culturally Diverse Democratic Societies*, Strasbourg: Council of Europe.

Cummins, J. (1997) 'Linguistic Interdependence and the Educational Development of Bilingual Children', *Review of Educational Research*, 49, 222–51.

Cummins, J. (2000) *Language, Power, and Pedagogy: Bilingual Children in the Crossfire*, Clevedon, UK: Multilingual Matters.

Cummins, J. (2013) 'Bilingual Education and Content and Language Integrated Learning (CLIL): Research and Its Classroom Implications', *Padres y Maestros*, February no. 349.

Cumming, J. and Lyster, R. (2016) 'Integrating CBI into High School Foreign Language Classrooms', in L. Cammarata (ed.), *Content-based Foreign Language Teaching: For Developing Advanced Thinking and Literacy*, New York, NY: Routledge, pp. 77–97.

Davison, C. and Williams, A. (2001) 'Integrating Language and Content: Unresolved Issues', in B. Mohan, C. Leung and C. Davison (eds.), *English as a Second Language in the Mainstream*, Harlow, UK: Pearson Education Ltd., pp. 51–70.

Deardorff, D. (2006) 'The Identification and Assessment of Intercultural Competence as a Student Outcome of Internationalization at Institutions of Higher Education in the United States', *Journal of Studies in International Education*, 10: 241–66.

Deardorff, D. (2013) *Promoting Understanding and Development of Intercultural Dialogue and Peace: A Comparative Analysis and Global Perspective of Regional Studies on Intercultural Competence*, Paris: UNESCO Division of Cultural Policies and Intercultural Dialogue.

Deardorff, D. K. (2014) *Some Thoughts on Assessing Intercultural Competence*. [https://illinois.edu/blog/view/915/113048, access date 11/06/2017].

Delors, J. (1993) *Letter to the European Schools, Reprinted in Schola Europaea: 1953–1993*, Brussels: European School.

Department for Education (2013) *The European Schools System*, London: DES.

Deleuze, G. (1968) *Différence et répétition* (Paris: PUF); translated as *Difference and Repetition*, by Paul Patton, New York: Columbia University Press.

Diderot, D. (ed.) (1751–72) Encyclopédie, or dictionnaire raisonné des sciences, des arts et des métiers (Encyclopaedia, or a Systematic Dictionary of the Sciences, Arts, and Crafts), www.

Erasmus, D. (2017) *Querela Pacis*, Reink: Books.

Laertius, Diogenes (1925a) 'The Cynics: Diogenes', *Lives of the Eminent Philosophers*, 2, 6, translated by Hicks, Robert Drew (two volume edition), Loeb Classical Library, 20–81.

Laertius, Diogenes (1925b) 'The Stoics: Zeno', *Lives of the Eminent Philosophers*, 2, 7, translated by Hicks, Robert Drew (two volume edition), Loeb Classical Library, 1–160.

Dore, R. (1976) *The Diploma Disease: Education, Qualification, and Development*, Berkeley: University of California Press.

Eccles, J. and Gootman, J. (eds.) (2002) *Community Programs to Promote Youth Development*, Washington, DC: National Academy Press.

Echevarria, J., Vogt, E. and Short, D. (2008) *Making Content Comprehensible for English Language Learners: The SIOP Model* (3rd edition), Boston: Allyn S Bacon.

Ellis, N. C. and Robinson, P. (2008) 'An Introduction to Cognitive Linguistics, Second Language Acquisition, and Language Instruction', in N. Ellis and P. Robinson (eds.), *Handbook of Cognitive Linguistics and Second Language Acquisition*, London: Routledge, pp. 3–24.

Engeström, Y. (2001) 'Expansive Learning at Work: Toward an Activity Theoretical Reconceptualization', *Journal of Education and Work*, 14, 1: 133–56.

European Commission (2003) *Promoting Language Learning and Linguistic Diversity: An Action Plan 2004–2006*. Brussels: European Commission.

European Commission (2005) *A New Framework Strategy for Multilingualism*. Brussels: European Commission.

European Commission (2007) *Final Report, High Level Group on Multilingualism*, Luxembourg: European Commission.

European Commission (2017) *New Narrative for Culture*. [https://ec.europa.eu/culture/policy/new-narrative, access date 11/06/2017].

European Community (1957) *Treaty Establishing the European Community, Rome, 25th March 1957*, Supplement No. 32 (1992), Brussels: European Community.

European Community (1964) *European Community* (70) April 1964, Washington, DC: European Community.

Evans, C. (2013) 'Making Sense of Assessment Feedback in Higher Education', *Review of Educational Research*, 83, 1: 70–120.

Fail, H., Thompson, J. and Walker, G. (2004) 'Belonging, Identity and Third Culture Kids: Life Histories of Former International School Students', *Journal of Research in International Education*, 3, 3: 319–338. https://doi.org/10.1177/1475240904047358.

Falchikov, N. (2001) *Learning Together: Peer Tutoring in Higher Education*, London: RoutledgeFalmer.

Finaldi-Baratieri, D. (2005) 'The "Only" European Schools in the European Union?', *European University Institute Working Papers*, HEC No. 2000/6.

Fogarty, R. (1991) *The Mindful School: How to Integrate the Curriculum*, Pallantine: Skylight Publishing.

Fortune, T. W. and Tedick, D. (2014) *Two-way Immersion* (Presentation), Tallinn: Estonia.
Fortune, T. W., Tedick, D. J. and Walker, C. L. (2008) 'Integrated Language and Content Teaching: Insights from the Immersion Classroom', in T. W. Fortune and D. J. Tedick (Eds.), *Pathways to Multilingualism: Evolving Perspectives on Immersion Education*, Clevedon: Multilingual Matters, pp. 71–96.
Foucault, M. (1972) 'The Discourse on Language (Appendix)', in M. Foucault (ed.), *Discipline and Punish: The Birth of the Prison*, New York: Random House.
Foucault, M. (1979) *Discipline and Punish: The Birth of the Prison*, New York: Vintage.
Foucault, M. (2004) *Security, Territory, Population: Lectures at the Collège de France 1977–1978*, New York: Picador Edition.
Fullan, M. (2001) *Leading in a Culture of Change*, San Francisco: Jossey-Bass.
Furedi, F. (2012) 'Putting Europe into Education', in J. Sayer and L. Erler (eds.), *Schools for the Future of Europe: Value and Change Beyond Lisbon*, London: Continuum.
Gagné, R. (1985) *The Conditions of Learning*, New York: Holt, Rinehart and Winston.
Gajo, L. (2007) 'Linguistic Knowledge and Subject Knowledge: How Does Bilingualism Contribute to Subject Development?', *International Journal of Bilingual Education and Bilingualism*, 10, 5: 563–81.
Garcia, S. and Wallace, H. (1993) 'Conclusion', in S. Garcia (ed.), *European Identity and the Search for Legitimacy*, London: Pinter.
Gardner, R. (1985) *Social Psychology and Second Language Learning: The Role of Attitudes and Motivation*, London: Edward Arnold.
General Secretary European Schools (2011) *Report*, European Schools Network.
Genesee, F. (2008) 'Dual Language in the Global Village', in T. W. Fortune and D. Tedick, (eds.), *Pathways to Multilingualism: Evolving Perspectives on Immersion Education*, Clevedon: Multilingual Matters, pp. 22–45.
Genesee, F. and Baetens Beardsmore, H. (2013) *Review of Research on Bilingual and Trilingual Education*, Astana: Nazarbayev Intellectual Schools.
Genesee, F. and Hamayan, E. (2016) *CLIL in Context Practical Guidance for Educators*, Cambridge: Cambridge University Press.
Gibbons, P. (2009) *English Learners, Academic Literacy and Thinking: Learning in the Challenge Zone*, Portsmouth, NH: Heinemann.
Goffman, E. (1963) *Stigma: Notes on the Management of Spoiled Identity*, New York: Prentice Hall.

Gray, J. (2003) 'Tense Conjugations: Translating Political Values into an Educational Model: The European Schools 1953–2003', *Journal of Research in International Education*, 2, 3: 315–30.

Gudykunst, W. B. (1993) 'Toward a Theory of Effective Interpersonal and Intergroup Communication: An Anxiety /Uncertainty Management (AUM) Perspective', in R. J. Wiseman and J. Koester (eds.), *Intercultural Communication Competence*, Thousand Oaks, CA: Sage, 3–71.

Haas, L. (2004) 'Schola Europea – The European School: The Fifteen-National School in Luxembourg: The Pedagogical Mini-Europe', *European Education*, 36, 3: 77–86.

Hacking, I. (1990) *The Taming of Chance*, Cambridge, MA: Harvard University Press.

Hannafin, M. J., Hannafin, K. D. and Dalton, D. W. (1993) 'Feedback and Emerging Instructional Technologies', in J. V. Dempsey and G. C. Sales (eds.), *Interactive Instruction and Feedback*, Englewood Cliffs, NJ: Educational Technology Publications, pp. 263–86.

Hansen, K. and Vignoles, A. (2005) 'The United Kingdom Education System in a Comparative Context', in S. Machin and A. Vignoles (eds.), *What's the Good of Education? The Economics of Education in the UK*, Princeton: Princeton University Press, pp. 13–35.

Harris, K. and Graham, S. (1999) 'Programmatic Intervention Research: Illustrations from the Evolution of Self-Regulated Strategy Development', *Learning Disability Quarterly*, 22: 251–62.

Hattie, J. (2008) *Visible Learning for Teachers*, London: Routledge.

Hattie, J. and Timperley, H. (2007) 'The Power of Feedback', *Review of Educational Research*, 77, 1: 81–112.

Hayden, M. and Thompson, J. (1997) 'Student Perspectives on International Education: A European Dimension', *Oxford Review of Education*, 23, 4: 459–78.

Heugh, K. (2016) 'Translanguaging as an Opportunity to Expand and Strengthen Students' Trilingual Repertoires', Presentation at the '*Trilingual Education: National and International Experience*' Conference Held in Astana, Kazakhstan 23–24 November.

Housen, A. (2002a) 'Processes and Outcomes in the European Schools Model of Multilingual Education', *Bilingual Research Journal*, 26, 1: 43–62.

Housen, A. (2002b) 'Second Language Achievement in the European School System of Multilingual Education', in D. So and G. Jones (eds.), *Education and Society in Plurilingual Contexts*, Brussels: VUB Press, pp. 96–128.

Housen, A. (2002c) 'Processes and Outcomes in the European Schools Model of Multilingual Education', *Bilingual Research Journal*, 26, 1: 43–62.
Housen, A. (2008) 'Multilingual Development in the European Schools', in R. De Groof (ed.), *Brussels and Europe – Bruxelles et l'Europe*, Brussels: Academic and Scientific Publishers, pp. 455–470.
Hu, M. and Nation, I. (2000) 'Vocabulary Density and Reading Comprehension', *Reading in a Foreign Language*, 13, 1: 403–30.
Interparents (2013) *Letter from Interparents Regarding the Funding Crisis at the European Schools*, Brussels: The Association of the Parents' Associations of the European Schools.
Janne, H. (1973) 'For a Community Policy on Education', *Bulletin of the European Communities*, Supplement 10/73, Brussels: European Commission.
Jenkins, S., Micklewright, J. and Schnepf, S. (2006) *Social Segregation in Secondary Schools: How Does England Compare with Other Countries?* Discussion Paper No. 1959 January 2006, Bonn: IZA.
Johnstone, R. (2002) *Immersion in a Second or Additional Language at School: A Review of the International Research*, Glasgow: CILT – Scotland's National Centre for Languages.
Jonckers, R. (2000) 'The European School Model Part II', *The European Schools Journal*, 20, 1, 1: 45–50.
Kaldor, M. (2003) 'The Idea of Global Civil Society', *International Affairs*, 79, 3: 583–93.
Kant, I. (1992) *The Cambridge Edition of the Works of Immanuel Kant*, edited by P. Guyer and A. Wood, 1992–, Cambridge: Cambridge University Press.
Kasper, G. (2008) 'Language', in J. Cenoz and N. H. Hornberger (eds.), *Encyclopedia of Language and Education*, 6, New York: Springer, pp. 59–78.
Kasper, G. and Rose, K. R. (2002) *Pragmatic Development in a Second Language*, Oxford: Blackwell.
Kegan, R. and Lahey, M. (2009) *Immunity to Change: How to Overcome It and Unlock the Potential in Yourself and Your Organization*, Boston: Harvard Business Press.
Kinstler, L. (2015) 'The European (Schools) Crisis', *Politico* 07/09/2015.
Kolb, D. (1984) *Experiential Learning Experience as a Source of Learning and Development*, New Jersey: Prentice Hall.
Lave, J. and Wenger, E. (1998) *Situated Learning: Legitimate Peripheral Participation*, Cambridge: Cambridge University Press.
Leaton Gray, S., Scott, D., Gutierrez-Peris, D., Mehisto, P., Pachler, N. and Reiss, M. (2015) *External Evaluation of a Proposal for the Reorganisation of*

Secondary Studies in the European School System, London: UCL Institute of Education.

Legenhausen, L. (2009) 'Autonomous Language Learning', in K. Knapp and B. Seidlhofer (eds.), *Handbook of Foreign Language Communication and Learning*, London: Mouton de Gruyter, pp. 373–400.

Lightbown, P. and Spada, N. (2013) *How Languages Are Learned* (4th edition), Oxford: Oxford University Press.

Little, O. and Boynton, L. (2004) *Personal Communication*.

Locke, J. (2007 [1689]) *An Essay Concerning Human Understanding*, London: Fontana Library.

Lyster, R. (2007) *Learning and Teaching Languages Through Content: A Counterbalanced Approach*, Philadelphia, PA: John Benjamins.

MacIntyre, P. (2002) 'Motivation, Anxiety and Emotion in Second Language Acquisition', in P. Robinson (ed.), *Individual Differences and Instructed Language Learning*, Philadelphia, PA: John Benjamins, pp. 45–68.

Marjoram, D. and Williams, R. (1977) 'European Schools: Based on an Agreement Between Nine Nations', *Trends in Education*, 2: 26–30.

Martel, J. (2016) 'Tapping the National Standards for Thought-Provoking CBI in K-16 Foreign Language Programs', in L. Cammarata (ed.), *Content-based Foreign Language Teaching: For Developing Advanced Thinking and Literacy*, New York, NY: Routledge, pp. 101–22.

Martinez, M., Hetterschijt, C. and Iglesias, M. (2015) 'The European Schools: Perspectives of Parents as Participants in a Learning Community', *Journal of Research in International Education*, 14, 1: 44–61.

Maton, K. (2014) *Knowledge and Knowers: Towards a Realist Sociology of Education*, London: Routledge.

McLaren, P. and Farahmandpur, R. (2001) 'The Globalization of Capitalism and the New Imperialism: Notes Towards a Revolutionary Critical Pedagogy', *The Review of Education, Pedagogy and Cultural Studies*, 23, 3: 271–315.

Meece, J., Anderman, E. and Anderman, L. (2006) 'Classroom Goal Structure, Student Motivation, and Academic Achievement', *Annual Review of Psychology*, 57, 1: 487–503.

Mehisto, P. (2012) *Excellence in Bilingual Education: A Guide for School Principals*, Cambridge: Cambridge University Press.

Mehisto, P. (2015) 'Conclusion: Forces, Mechanisms and Counterweights', in P. Mehisto and F. Genesee (eds.), *Building Bilingual Education Systems: Forces, Mechanisms and Counterweights*, Cambridge: Cambridge University Press, pp. 269–88.

Mehisto, P. with Ting, T. (2017) *CLIL Essentials for Secondary School Teachers*. Cambridge: Cambridge University Press.

Mercer, N. and Dawes, L. (2008) 'The Value of Exploratory Talk', in N. Mercer and S. Hodgkinson (eds.), *Exploring Talk in Schools*, London: Sage, pp. 55–71.

Messick, S. (1989) 'Validity', in R. Linn (ed.), *Educational Measurement* (3rd edition), Washington, DC: American Council on Education.

Meyer, E. (2014) *Navigating the Cultural Minefield*, Harvard University Press.

Mourshed, M., Chijioke, C. and Barber, M. (2010) *How the World's Best Performing Systems Come Out on Top*, London: McKinsey.

Murphy, V. (2016) 'Research on Raising Achievement in English Language and/or Literacy in Pupils with EAL', Presentation at the '*Multilingual Learners in Context – EAL, Community and International School Settings*' Symposium Held at Oxford Brookes University, Oxford, 11 June.

National Academies of Sciences, Engineering, and Medicine (2017) *Promoting the Educational Success of Children and Youth Learning English: Promising Futures*, Washington, DC: The National Academies Press.

Nelson, M. and Schunn, C. (2009) 'The Nature of Feedback: How Different Types of Peer Feedback Affect Writing Performance', *Instructional Science*, 27, 4: 375–401.

Nic Craith, M. (2006) *Europe and the Politics of Language: Citizens, Migrants and Outsiders*, Palgrave Studies in Minority Languages and Communities, Basingstoke: Palgrave Macmillan.

OECD (2016) *Education 2030: Preliminary Reflections and Research by Experts on Knowledge, Skills, Attitudes and Values towards 2030*, Paris: OECD.

Office of Secretary General of the European Schools (2017) Statistics, https://www.eursc.eu/en.

Office of Secretary General of the European Schools (2016) Statistics, https://www.eursc.eu/en.

Olsen, J. (2000) 'The European School Model Part I', *The International Schools Journal*, 20, 1: 38–44.

Oostlander, A. (1993) *Report on the Proposal for a Council Decision on the Conclusion by the European Economic Community and the European Atomic Energy Community of the Convention Defining the Statute of the European Schools* (com 93- c3-0142/93), Brussels: Europ 26262 Session Documents.

Osberg, D. and Biesta, G. (2007) 'Beyond Presence: Epistemological and Pedagogical Implications of Strong Emergence', *Interchange*, 38, 1: 31–51.

Osler, A. and Starkey, H. (2005) *Changing Citizenship: Democracy and Inclusion in Education*, Maidenhead: Open University Press.

Parker, R. (1985) 'The "Language Across the Curriculum" Movement: A Brief Overview and Bibliography', *College Composition and Communication*, 36, 2: 173–7.

Pomerantsev, P. (2016) 'European Schools', *London Review of Books*, 38, 12: 46–7.

Reagan, T. (2016) 'Language Teachers in Foreign Territory: A Call for a Critical Pedagogy-Infused Curriculum', in L. Cammarata (ed.), *Content-Based Foreign Language Teaching: For Developing Advanced Thinking and Literacy*, New York, NY: Routledge, 173–91.

Ruiz de Zarobe, Y. (2015) 'The Basque Country: Plurilingual Education', in P. Mehisto and F. Genesee (eds.), *Building Bilingual Education Systems: Forces Mechanisms and Counterweights*, Cambridge: Cambridge University Press.

Rydenvald, M. (2015) 'Elite Bilingualism? Language Use Among Multilingual Teenagers of Swedish Background in European Schools and International Schools in Europe', *Journal of Research in International Education*, 14, 3: 213–27.

Savvides, N. (2006a) 'Developing a European Identity: A Case Study of the European School at Culham', *Comparative Education*, 42, 1: 113–29.

Savvides, N. (2006b) 'Investigating Education for European Identity at Three European Schools: A Research Proposal', *Research in Comparative and International Education*, 1, 2: 174–86.

Savvides, N. (2006c) 'Comparing the Promotion of European Identity at Three 'European Schools': An Analysis of Teachers' Perceptions', *Research in Comparative and International Education*, 1, 4: 393–402.

Savvides, N. (2008) 'The European Dimension in Education: Exploring Students' Perceptions at Three European Schools', *Journal of Research in International Education*, 7, 3: 304–26.

Schleicher, A. (2013) www.bbc.com/news/business-31087545.

Schmalenbach, K. (2010) 'Challenging Decisions of the European Schools Before National Courts', in A. Reinisch (ed.), *Challenging Acts of International Organizations Before National Courts*, Oxford: Oxford University Press.

Scott, D. (2011) *Education, Epistemology and Critical Realism*, London and New York: Routledge.

Schon, D. (2005) *The Reflective Practitioner: How Professionals Think in Action*, San Francisco: Jossey Bass.

Shapiro, B. (1994) *What Children Bring to Light: A Constructivist Perspective on Children's Learning in Science*, New York: Teachers College Press.

Shore, C. and Baratieri, D. (2005) 'Crossing Boundaries Through Europe: European Schools and the Supersession of Nationalism', in J. Stacul,

C. Moutsou and H. Kopnina (eds.), *Crossing European Boundaries: Beyond Conventional Geographical Categories*, Oxford: Berghahn Books.

Shore, C. and Finaldi, D. (2005) 'Crossing Boundaries Through Education: European Schools and the Supersession of Nationalism', in J. Stacul et al. (eds.), *Crossing European Boundaries Beyond Conventional Geographical Categories*, Berghahn Books, pp. 23–40.

Smith, A. (1995) 'The Special Needs of Gifted Children in the European Schools', *Schola Europaea*, Brussels: European School.

Spitzberg, B. H. and Changnon, G. (2009) 'Conceptualizing Multicultural Competence', in D. K. Deardorff (ed.), *Handbook of Intercultural Competence*, Thousand Oaks, CA: Sage, 2–52.

Stacul, J., Moutsou, C. and Kopnina, H. (2006) *Crossing European Boundaries: Beyond Conventional Geographic Categories*, New York: Berghahn Books.

Standish, P. (2016) 'The Disenchantment of Education and the Re-enchantment of the World', *Journal of Philosophy of Education*, 50, 1: 98–116.

Starkey, H. (2012) 'Europe, Human Rights and Education', in J. Sayer and L. Erler (eds.), *Schools for the Future of Europe Values and Change Beyond Lisbon*, London: Continuum.

Strawson, P. (1959) *Individuals: An Essay in Descriptive Metaphysics*, London: Methuen.

Swan, D. (1996) *A Singular Pluralism: The European Schools 1984–94*, Dublin: Institute of Public Administration.

Tedick, D. J. and Wesely, P. M. (2015) 'A Review of Research on Content-Based Foreign/Second Language Education in US K-12 Contexts', *Language, Culture and Curriculum*, 28, 1: 25–40,

Theiler, T. (1999) 'The European Union and the 'European Dimension' in Schools: Theory and Evidence', *Journal of European Integration*, 21, 4: 307–41.

UNESCO (2001) *Universal Declaration on Cultural Diversity*, November 2001.

Van Dijk Consultants (2006) *Evaluation of the European Schools at Culham, Mol, Bergen and Karlsruhe and Options for the Future*, 17 of August 2006, Brussels: Van Dijk Consultants.

Van Parijs, P. (2009) *Linguistic Justice for Europe*, Oxford: Oxford University Press.

Vollmer, H. J. (2006) *Language Across the Curriculum*, Strasbourg: Council of Europe.

Vygotsky, L. S. (1978) *Mind in Society: The Development of Higher Psychological Processes*, Cambridge, MA: Harvard University Press.

Watson, A., Jones, K. and Pratt, D. (2013) *Key Ideas in Teaching Mathematics: Research-Based Guidance for Ages 9–19*, Oxford: Oxford University Press.

Wiliam, D. and Thompson, M. (2008) 'Integrating Assessment with Instruction: What Will It Take to Make It Work?', in C. Dwyer (ed.), *The Future of Assessment: Shaping Teaching and Learning*, Mawah, NJ: Lawrence Erlbaum Associates, pp. 53–82.

Williams, C. (1996) 'Secondary Education: Teaching in the Bilingual Situation', in C. Williams, G. Lewis and C. Baker (eds.), *The Language Policy: Taking Stock*, Llangefni, Wales: CAI.

Wilson, E. and Demetrio, H. (2007) 'New Teacher Learning: Substantive Knowledge and Contextual Factors', *The Curriculum Journal*, 18, 3: 213–29.

Wolff, D. (2011) 'The CLIL Teacher's Strategic Competence', Presentation Given at '*International CLIL Conference: Towards Quality CLIL Teaching*' Held in Rovereto, Italy, Centro Rovereto on 19 February.

Zimmerman, B. and Schunk, D. (2011) *Handbook of Self-regulation of Learning and Performance*, New York: Routledge.

Author Index

A

Allemann-Ghionda, C., 32, 56
Ansell, C., 82
Appiah, A., 144
Argyris, C., 20
Aubrey, B., 147

B

Baetens Beardsmore, H., 9, 66, 81, 92
Baker, C., 71
Ball, S., 85
Bandura, A., 146
Banks, J. A., 32, 57, 139
Baratieri, D., 76, 80, 84, 92
Bernstein, B., 47, 48, 131, 153, 154
Biesta, G., 19
Black, P., 149

Bolton, G., 149
Bourdieu, P., 65
Boynton, L., 71
Brandom, R., 46, 47, 149
Bridges, D., 152
Brinton, D., 62
Bruner, J., 26
Bullock, A., 66
Bulmer, J., 9
Bulwer, J., 80, 91, 92

C

Cammarata, L., 51, 61, 62
Candelier, M., 58, 59, 69
Carlos, S., 76, 82
Chamot, A., 65
Cloud, N., 52
Clutterbuck, D., 147

Cohen, P., 147
Collins, A., 146
Cummins, J., 51, 71

D

Davison, C., 62
Deardorff, D., 58
Deleuze, G., 128
Delors, J., 7
Demetrio, H., 150
Dore, R., 112

E

Eccles, J., 56
Echevarria, J., 65
Ellis, N., 51, 65

F

Falchikov, N., 148
Farahmandpur, R., 143
Finaldi-Baratieri, D., 14
Fogarty, R., 153
Fortune, T., 52
Foucault, M., 109, 110
Fullan, M., 20, 52
Furedi, F., 95

G

Gagné, R., 149
Gajo, L., 52
Garcia, S., 78
Gardner, R., 67
Genesee, F., 51, 52, 65, 66, 71
Gibbons, P., 64, 65
Goffman, E., 94

Gootman, J., 56
Graham, S., 150
Gray, J., 81
Gutierrez-Peris, D., xi

H

Haas, L., 77, 93
Hacking, I., 18
Hamayan, E., 51, 65, 71
Hannafin, M., 156
Hansen, K., 128, 129
Harris, K., 150
Hattie, J., 83, 156
Hayden, M., 76, 90
Heugh, K., 71
Housen, A., 66
Hu, M., 65

J

Janne, H., 79
Jenkins, S., 85
Johnstone, R., 66
Jonckers, R., 77

K

Kaldor, M., 140
Kasper, G., 65
Kegan, R., 21
Kinstler, L., 77
Kohls, J., 81, 92

L

Lahey, M., 21
Leaton Gray, S., xi, 22, 56, 61, 81, 107
Legenhausen, L., 67

Author Index   177

Lightbown, P., 62
Little, O., 71
Locke, J., 141
Lyster, R., 61, 66

M
MacIntyre, P., 67
Marjoram, D., 94
Martel, J., 52, 61
Martinez, M., 83
Maton, K., 47
McLaren, P., 143
Meece, J., 147
Megginson, D., 147
Mehisto, P., xi, 51, 60, 67
Messick, S., 113, 117
Meyer, E., 58
Mourshed, M., 117
Murphy, V., 65

N
Nation, I., 65
Nelson, M., 156
Nic Craith, M., 80

O
O'Malley, J., 65
Oostlander, A., 89
Osberg, D., 19
Osler, A., 95

P
Pachler, N., xi
Parker, R., 66

Passeron, J.-C., 65
Plowright, D., 149
Pomerantsev, P., 93, 95

R
Reagan, T., 63
Reiss, M., xi
Robinson, P., 51, 65
Rose, K., 65
Ruiz de Zarobe, Y., 69
Rydenvald, M., 77

S
Savvides, N., 8, 9, 76, 78, 81, 92, 95
Schleicher, A., 112
Schmalenbach, K., 90
Schunk, D., 146
Schunn, C., 156
Scott, D., xi, 18, 20
Shapiro, B., 33
Shore, C., 8, 9, 12, 76, 80, 84, 92
Smith, A., 9
Spada, N., 62
Stacul, J., 90
Starkey, H., 81, 88, 95
Swan, D., 9, 11, 12, 94

T
Tedick, D., 52, 62
Theiler, T., 76, 81, 92
Thompson, J., 76, 90
Thompson, M., 145
Timperley, H., 156
Ting, T., 67

V
Van Dijk Consultants, 16
Van Parijs, P., 122, 129
Vignoles, A., 128, 129
Vollmer, H., 66
Vygotsky, L., 65

W
Wallace, H., 78
Watson, A., 32

Wiliam, D., 145
Williams, A., 62
Williams, C., 70
Williams, R., 94
Wilson, E., 150
Wolff, D., 64

Z
Zimmerman, B., 146

Subject Index

A

Access, vii, 2, 7, 14–16, 23, 29, 46, 76, 79, 88, 90, 106, 107, 121–125, 136
Admission, 14–16, 36, 85–89, 96, 105, 121–128
Assessment, vi, viii, 1, 3, 21, 23, 25, 26, 48, 53, 54, 64, 69, 70, 72, 79, 99–119, 121, 144, 145, 151, 154, 156–158
Autonomy, 3, 8, 67, 104

B

Baccalaureate, 5–7, 11, 29, 31, 35, 36, 44, 99–101, 104, 105, 108, 109, 119, 126–128
  European, 2, 5–7, 17, 18, 26, 29, 31, 36, 46, 76, 81, 94, 96, 99, 102–109, 111, 119, 121, 124, 126–128, 131, 132, 136, 139, 158

Belgium, v, 5, 95, 99
Board of Governors, v, 6–10, 16, 29–32, 34, 35, 44, 78, 82, 85, 86, 88, 102, 105, 107, 122
Bureaucracy, 129

C

Capacity, vii, 2, 3, 9, 21, 25, 26, 28, 46, 51, 55, 61, 107, 114, 118, 144, 146, 150, 152
Change, v, 2–4, 18–21, 27, 30, 46, 54, 64, 124, 143, 147, 157
  catalyst, 2
Citizenship, 9, 30, 75, 81, 93–96, 139–141, 143, 144
Communication
  competence, 68
  cross-cultural, 68
Complexity, 19, 27, 28, 47, 82
Cosmopolitanism, 137, 140–144
Council of Europe, 55, 60, 66

Subject Index

Curriculum, v, 1, 5, 23–27, 29–31, 33, 34, 36–38, 40–44, 46, 47, 49, 76, 99, 121, 139
   reform, vii, 34, 46–48

D

Department for Education (DfE), 126, 127
Didactics, 24

E

Economics, 5, 9, 11, 31, 32, 36, 39, 40, 42, 43, 50, 62, 81, 100, 102, 132, 133, 135
Education
   higher, vi, 21, 29, 35, 38, 46, 119, 121–126, 128–134, 136, 137
   intercultural, 32, 56
   multicultural, 32, 52–54, 58
   religious, 37, 130
   system, 2–4, 20, 21, 23, 35, 51, 52, 58, 65, 70, 76, 78, 87, 89, 107, 109, 113, 116–119, 125, 129, 139
Emergence, 19, 20, 142
Erasmus, 124, 142
Europe, viii, 1, 6, 9, 14, 16, 30, 31, 54, 55, 60, 66, 75–96, 110, 119, 124, 125, 131, 134, 142
European
   Baccalaureate, 2, 5–7, 17, 18, 26, 29, 31, 36, 46, 76, 81, 94, 96, 99, 102–109, 111, 119, 121, 124, 126–128, 131, 132, 136, 139, 158
   category I, 5–8, 10, 16, 85, 88, 122
   category II, 5–7, 77, 85, 86, 122
   category III, 5–7, 12, 16, 77, 85–88
   commission, 8, 22, 34, 55, 56, 77, 78, 82, 122, 124
   school, v, vi, viii, 1–23, 25, 27, 29, 33, 48, 52, 83, 85, 87, 90, 93–95, 99, 115–117, 119, 125, 127, 144, 151, 158
   schooling, 6, 7, 29, 30, 83, 91
   system, 157
   Union, v, 1, 4, 6, 8, 10–12, 14, 17, 30, 31, 34, 56, 78, 79, 82, 89, 95, 102, 105, 130, 131, 158
European Atomic Energy Commission, 5
European Coal and Steel Community, 4
European Commission (EC), 8, 22, 26, 34, 55, 56, 76–78, 82, 122, 124
European Economic Community, 5, 157
Examination, 7, 18, 25, 44, 81, 94, 96, 101–104, 106–113, 118, 119, 125, 128, 130, 141

G

Gaignage criteria, 10
General Secretary European Schools, v, 5, 6, 13, 15, 18, 90, 96
Geography, 9, 11, 12, 14, 31, 32, 36–44, 56, 62, 64, 76, 95, 102, 106, 132, 133, 135
Germany, 5, 11, 95

Subject Index

H
History, 1–22, 31, 32, 35, 36, 38–44, 49, 50, 56, 57, 62, 76, 95, 102, 117, 126, 133, 135, 139, 142, 144

I
Ideology, 76, 95
International, 3, 14, 17, 75, 76, 80, 88, 89, 92, 93, 95, 96, 99, 100, 116–118, 121, 124, 129, 141–144
Interparents, 30, 82, 91
Italy, 5, 36, 95

K
Knowledge, vii, 4, 9, 18, 20, 21, 23–27, 29, 32, 34–36, 38, 39, 41, 46, 47, 51, 52, 55–61, 63, 65, 68, 70, 72, 81, 96, 102, 103, 108, 110, 113, 114, 127, 129, 136, 143, 147, 149–157

L
Language
  awareness, 67, 68
  curriculum, 63
  instruction, 69–72
  learning skills, 68
  pluralism, 11
  policy, 9, 11, 12, 14, 18, 50–54, 72
Latin, 36, 37, 42, 43, 132, 135
Learning
  coaching, 25
  concept-formation, 25
  environment, 24
  goal-orientated, 25
  instruction, 25
  mentoring, 25
  meta-cognitive, 25
  observation, 25
  peer, 25
  practice, 25
  problem-solving, 25
  reflection, 25
  simulation, 25
Leavers, 84, 121, 123
Luxembourg, 1, 4, 5, 7–11, 13, 16, 83, 87, 95, 132, 134, 158

M
Management of Change, 21
Mother tongue, vi, 5, 6, 9, 11, 12, 30, 32, 34, 40, 56, 65, 70, 77, 87, 91, 92, 127, 139, 158
Multiculturalism, 70
Multilingualism, 18, 32, 53, 55, 56, 69, 70, 72

N
National Academies of Sciences, Engineering, and Medicine, 65, 66
Nationality, 12, 13, 56, 124, 144
Needs
  emotional, 2
  intellectual, 2
  material, 2
  spiritual, 2
The Netherlands, 5, 78, 95

O

Office of the Secretary General of the European Schools, 5, 6, 13, 15, 18, 82, 88
Opening up, 2, 6, 7, 29
Option, 11, 17, 28, 31, 36–38, 40–44, 63, 102, 103, 108
Organization for Economic Cooperation and Development (OECD), 3, 112, 115

P

Pedagogy, viii, 9, 17, 30, 32, 52, 63, 70, 72, 92, 139, 153
Philosophy, 31, 36–40, 43, 44, 81, 89, 100, 102, 132, 133, 140, 142, 149
Population, 6–8, 10, 12, 13, 15, 16, 44, 53, 113, 114, 122, 126, 129, 134, 154
Probability, 18, 135
Programme for International Student Assessment (PISA), 3, 112, 114

R

Reform, v–viii, 2, 4, 6, 8, 16, 20, 21, 28, 31, 33, 34, 41, 46–50, 52, 77, 81, 99–119, 132, 136, 158
Repeaters, 121, 123
Research, viii, 22, 32, 63, 67, 68, 71, 72, 84, 93, 101, 117, 118, 121, 124, 126

S

Schools
  Category 1, 10, 11, 16, 125
  Category 2, 125
  Category 3, 89
Second foreign language, 9
Segregation, 72, 75, 82–93
Selection, 2, 35, 72, 75, 82–93, 115, 118, 122, 127, 130
Social Striations
  dis(ability), 128
  gender, 128
  intelligence, 128
  race, 128
  sexuality, 128
  social class, 128
Sociology, 38–40, 43, 75–96, 132
Sorting, 72, 75, 82–93
Spain, 5, 36, 99
Students without a Language Section (SWALS), 10, 12, 18, 50, 70, 91, 158
Subject, 28, 33–38, 41–45, 50, 56, 57, 61, 64–70, 77, 81, 83, 95, 100–104, 106, 108–110, 126, 127, 129, 132, 142, 152, 157, 158
System, v, 2, 23, 50, 75, 121, 139

T

Textbook, 14, 92
Third foreign language, 31
Time, v, viii, 2, 3, 5, 9, 11, 16–20, 22, 26, 33, 35, 36, 38, 41, 45, 47, 54, 57, 66, 75, 78, 79, 82, 83, 92, 93, 96, 101,

104, 106, 110, 112, 115, 117, 122, 123, 125, 129–131, 139, 141, 142, 146, 148, 150, 151, 153, 156

U

UNESCO, 57
United Kingdom, 5, 17
University, v–vii, 17, 22, 34–36, 38, 41, 100, 105–107, 121, 123–129, 131, 132, 134

Use, 1, 8, 12, 18, 52, 53, 55, 57, 59–72, 80, 83, 88, 93, 101–103, 105, 107, 111–113, 115–119, 146, 147, 150, 152, 156

V

Validity, 106, 116–119

W

Working Language, 11, 12, 14, 31

The manufacturer's authorised representative in the EU is Springer Nature Customer Service Centre GmbH, Europaplatz 3, 69115 Heidelberg, Germany. If you have any concerns regarding our products, please contact ProductSafety@springernature.com

Printed and bound by CPI Group (UK) Ltd, Croydon, CR0 4YY
23/03/2026
02076683-0002